I BET THE FARM

An Arran farmer's European odyssey

Sandy MacAlister

Dedication

In memory of my brother Charlie tragically lost February 2025

Blues for Charlie

Copyright Phil Barling – March 2025

A quiet man, Charlie — a man of few words

Yet those spoken were heartfelt and strong.

We celebrate the brother, the father, the friend:

Come by, away, walk on.

A humble man, Charlie — solitary, maybe,

But not lonely, he'd have you know.

At home with his dogs and his blues,

Working tirelessly through rain, wind and snow.

Tomorrow, as sun rises o'er yonder hill,

And this sad blues has ended and gone,

There'll be a stillness tonight in the valley:

Come by, away, walk on.

But today, blues pours on us like rain.

Quietness falls over field, glen and town,

Save for the farmer's distant call:

Come by, away, lie down.

Glossary

The Common Periwinkle

Littorina littorea

Also known as:

Winkles

Wilks (Scots)

Bigorneau (French)

Bigaro (Spanish)

Chapter 1:

Autumn 1985

My entry into the world of shellfish came purely by accident, the result of a misunderstood throwaway comment.

We had just endured the wettest summer anyone could remember—certainly the wettest I had ever seen—and I had six acres of potatoes needing lifted. By the end of September, I was in despair as to how I would ever get them out of the ground, when, miraculously, the weather suddenly changed. A spell of East wind set in, beginning to dry the sodden ground. As luck would have it, it was the heaviest clay on the farm and so took the longest to dry out.

However, going by the forecast, it should be dry enough to get on the ground with a tractor and digger for a few days by about mid-October, I thought. But that raised the next problem—who was I going to get to gather (sometimes called "pick") the potatoes?

My thoughts turned to the travelling folk on the site at Merkland Point, and I went there to see who I could find for the job.

I drove into the site, a place I had never been before, to be met by half a dozen or so men and teenage boys standing around, chatting and drinking tea. As I got out of the car, one of them came over, and I explained why I was there.

"What sort of money would be involved?" he asked. I told him.

At this, he shook his head. "No, I don't think any of the boys would be interested," he said. "But I'll ask them anyway." Which he did. There was a unanimous shaking of heads.

I threw in what I hoped would be a difference-maker. "It would all be cash."

Still no interest.

Intrigued by the lack of enthusiasm from folk obviously with time on their hands, I asked, "What do you folk do? For money, I mean?"

"Well, everybody here goes to the tide," came the reply.

Puzzled, I asked, "What does that mean? What's involved in going to the tide?"

"Picking wilks," was the answer.

"Ah, I see." I had seen people out on the shore from time to time collecting wilks into bags, though I had never given it much thought. "Right, well, what about in between the tides? Would anybody give it a go then?"

I upped the hourly rate and eventually got a promise that some of the lads would come over the next day we were gathering, provided it didn't happen at the same time as low tide—the prime time for gathering wilks.

As I was getting back into the car, the first guy I had spoken to said, "Do you know anything about exporting?"

"A wee bit," I replied, thinking he meant exporting from the island to the mainland, as we had recently sent Brussels sprouts to Glasgow Fruit Market.

"If you do, there's a fortune to be made exporting these wilks to France and Spain," he said. "We sell to Uncle, and he's made a fortune from wilks."

I would eventually discover that every wilk picker in Scotland believes the man he sells them to makes a fortune off their picking.

My name is Sandy MacAlister, and at that time, in 1985, I was farming sheep and cattle with my brother Charlie in the Shiskine Valley on the island of Arran in the Firth of Clyde.

Over the past few years, in partnership with our wives, Jan and Glynis, we had diversified the business. Like many farmers then— and now—I was asset rich but cash poor, and I was fed up with the second part of that equation.

First, we renovated a couple of holiday cottages and started a riding holidays venture. Then we began growing vegetables to sell around the island and through a farm shop, we had started, later adding fruit from the Glasgow Fruit Market to the products we were growing and selling.

The riding holidays were run in conjunction with bed and breakfast guests, with the horse riders and B&B guests staying in our house. Our house—a five-bedroom farmhouse with dining room, living room, and kitchen—only had one bathroom, which was a bit of a problem considering there were often ten or more people sleeping in the house.

Jan and I were also bringing up three children at the time. The distribution of the bedrooms—one for our daughters Katie (10) and Louise (8), one for our son John (12), and three for the paying guests—meant Jan and I slept on a mattress on the living room floor from May until October.

At that time, in the late seventies and early eighties, the quality of vegetables in the island's shops was pretty ordinary, as most of it came from the Glasgow Fruit Market. By the time it arrived, it was days old and often tired-looking. I was sure we could do better on our farm by cutting down the time from field to shop—or hotel—from days to just a few hours.

So I sowed cabbages and turnips and planted potatoes with a view to selling them to shops, hotels, and restaurants around the island.

For a farmer, that was the easy bit. The hard part was knocking on the doors of almost every hotel, shop, and restaurant on the island, introducing myself, and trying to persuade the proprietors to try our veg.

The response was fairly positive, though initially I was hindered by the fact that all I had to sell in the immediate future (late spring) were cabbages and turnips, as the potatoes wouldn't be ready for a few more weeks. There is a limit to the amount of cabbages and turnips required at that time of year.

However, undaunted, I went out one day, cut half a dozen bags of cabbages—the turnips were still not quite ready—loaded them into the back of my Ford Escort Estate, and set off for Brodick, Lamlash, and Whiting Bay, the three largest villages on the island.

I returned happy—without the cabbages, but with a few pounds in my pocket instead.

As someone who had rarely been out of Shiskine in the past few years—and in light of subsequent events—it sometimes amused me to recall that my biggest worry before I set off that day was:

What will I do if I break down in Whiting Bay?

About 16 miles away from the farm.

I knew we had to extend the range of veg we were growing but felt I didn't know enough about anything other than what we already had—traditional stock-feeding veg. So I looked around and found a vegetable grower in the Clyde Valley who sold vegetable plants in peat blocks (seedlings planted in peat blocks in trays and left to germinate in a greenhouse), ready to be planted out and grown on.

We planted broccoli, cauliflower, Brussels sprouts, courgettes, and lettuce, all of which grew well. By our second year, it was all systems go.

We had opened the farm shop, and by late spring we had lettuce—brought forward by covering the plants with plastic sheeting—soon followed by cauliflower and broccoli, all planted in sequence, timed (hopefully) to give a constant supply through summer and autumn.

To distinguish our veg from the opposition, I printed labels with the words **"Arran Fresh"** to be used by anyone selling our produce.

I soon received my first lesson in business-to-business trading, which, in my farmer's naivety, I hadn't anticipated.

Farmers, by and large—especially stock farmers—are price takers, not price makers. That is to say, they usually sell their stock at auction and must accept whatever price the market gives them. That price depends on many factors but is essentially a reflection of supply and demand at the time of sale.

Technically, the farmer can withdraw his stock if unhappy with the price offered, but that rarely happens—unless the trade is extremely poor. More often than not, he's depending on the sale to pay bills or reduce his overdraft, which he's probably just assured his bank manager will be done imminently.

I once withdrew stirks (yearling cattle) from Brodick Market after being offered just £5 each—only to sell them a few months later for not much more. I'd probably have been better off taking the fiver.

Anyway, if I'd thought about it at all, I probably imagined that the guys in Glasgow—once they realised their vegetable sales to

Arran were disappearing—would concede that they couldn't compete with the freshness and quality I was supplying.

Instead, three things happened at once:

1. The quality of veg sent down from Glasgow dramatically improved—amazingly, this happened despite prices *falling*.

2. The price of fruit like tomatoes, apples, oranges, melons, etc., suddenly went *up*, at a time of year when they would normally come down.

In hindsight, I should have ignored it and let them do their thing. But my competitive spirit wouldn't allow that. I saw it as a challenge—and one I would meet head-on.

I should have realised that we, as a family, were already stretched to the limit. But I was too young and inexperienced to understand that, in this instance, discretion would have been the better part of valour.

Our life at that point, from May to October, was a non-stop carousel of work.

Jan and I would be up by 6 a.m., have a cup of coffee, then head to the veg fields—cutting and boxing lettuce, cauliflower, and broccoli while battling midges and/or rain until around 8.

Jan would then head back to prepare breakfast for the B&B and riding holiday guests, while I loaded the veg into the van I'd bought for £120 at the Glasgow Motor Auction (which had only made it to the Gorbals before the gearbox fell out).

We'd both grab breakfast around 9. I'd set off on the veg delivery round by 9:30, while Jan cleared up after the guests. Glynis would fetch and prepare the horses for the day's ride, and Charlie would be tending sheep and cattle—or doing whatever the veg needed: ploughing, spraying, working the ground, or loading up produce picked that day by the workers we'd hired.

I usually got back around 4 p.m. to clean the van and load up the freshly harvested veg. Jan would prepare dinner for the guests while I phoned around for the next day's orders and worked out what more we'd need in the morning.

Adding fruit from Glasgow to that schedule was a step too far. Initially, I picked it up myself, but eventually contracted Bannatyne Motors, our local hauliers, to do the job.

So, by the time the wet summer of 1985 arrived, we'd had several years of this hectic lifestyle—and the strain was beginning to tell. Jan's health had suffered and although our diversifications were profitable, the lifestyle they required was clearly unsustainable.

That's why, when I started thinking about the possibilities in the winkle business, it seemed like a more manageable alternative—although I never imagined it would eventually reach the scale it did.

When I returned home from my visit to the travellers' site, I began to process what I had learned at Merkland.

Firstly—and most importantly—nobody was desperate for work lifting tatties. So I would have to make the remuneration attractive enough to tempt some of the travellers to come.

Otherwise, I was looking at an expensive disaster: a field full of potatoes, most of which would never be gathered.

But I was also intrigued by what I had been told about wilks, so I resolved to do some research on the subject whenever I had time.

This was in the days before the internet—when "to google" was to bowl an exotic delivery in a game of cricket—and information on obscure subjects was extremely difficult to obtain.

Essentially, what I had to do was find out all I could about a product I knew nothing about, which I would then buy to sell to people I had never met, in a country I knew nothing about, probably in a language of which I had only the flimsiest grasp, possibly in a foreign currency, and without knowing the market price for buying or selling.

But I did a bit of digging around and asking about, and discovered that there was a haulage company—A & J Logan—in Kilbirnie, about 40 minutes away from Ardrossan. They didn't buy winkles, but they *did* transport them to France for a French firm called Primel, located in Brittany.

So I phoned Logans and spoke to Ian Logan, who was very helpful and gave me the name and phone number of the buyer at Primel. He said that if I made a deal with Primel, they would likely get in touch with him, and he would then let me know when to bring the winkles to his yard.

That was the easy bit done.

The next step was to check whether the travellers would actually sell me their winkles. So when they arrived to gather tatties, I got confirmation that, for a better price than they were currently getting, they would—following the next big tide. Which meant that, notionally at least, I had something to sell.

The next step—and by far the most difficult one so far—was to call Primel and try to get a commitment to buy the winkles at a price that would leave me a profit.

Before doing that, I did some revision of my school French, as I wasn't sure how much English the Primel buyer spoke. So, with much trepidation, I dialled the number I'd been given.

It was actually the first time I had ever called a foreign number, and I was nervous as hell—because by that point I had already convinced myself there was a real opportunity here, and I didn't want to blow it before I'd even got started.

I asked to speak to the winkle buyer in my best school French, and he came on the line.

I needn't have worried—his English was better than my French—and I told him what I could supply. He wanted to know which area of Scotland the winkles were from and then told me what he would pay, if they were all in good condition.

I assured him they would be, and he said to let Logans know when I had them. They would tell me when to bring them to Kilbirnie. He'd receive them a couple of days later, and I would be paid at the end of that week.

So it was that about a week later, I went over to Merkland with a load of hay for a horse owner in Corrie and a pocketful of cash. I bought half a ton of winkles, and the next day took them to Logans at Kilbirnie.

I washed out the van, then went to the Glasgow Fruit Market, loaded up with fruit for my fruit and veg round, and was back home by 5 p.m.—sure that I could make a lot more of the winkle business with a bit more time and application.

Though, as ever, time continued to be at a premium.

Chapter 2:

I set out to find out what other winkle pickers there might be on the island, and who they were selling to.

As best as I could ascertain, there were about a dozen or so other people regularly or occasionally picking—supplemented by various groups of travelling folk who came to the island intermittently, mostly in summer. There were also some folk who came over from Kintyre in boats, stayed a few days, then went home, taking their winkles with them.

There were, at that time, three other buyers on the island.

To make this work, I thought, I needed to be able to offer these buyers a good enough price to make it worth their while to sell to me, rather than—as they currently did—to merchants on mainland Scotland. It wouldn't work if I tried to compete with them to buy directly off their pickers. I would make less on each bag, but would be handling a lot more bags—so it would be more profitable overall.

But to do that, I needed a better selling price.

So I reasoned—albeit not quite accurately—that Primel were probably selling in Paris, which logically (I thought) would be the best market in France. The fish market there was at Rungis, which I figured was the place to go and seek out a buyer a level up—someone who might offer a better price, one that would allow me to buy all the winkles on the island without going to war with the existing buyers.

I made enquiries about flying to Paris to visit Rungis, which is actually a huge enterprise claiming to be the biggest fresh food market in the world, where fruit and veg, meat, and all kinds of foodstuffs are sold—along with fish and shellfish.

From Glasgow, I could fly either British Airways or Air France. Both wanted around £650 return (£2007 at 2025 prices), unless you stayed over a Saturday night—in which case, one of them would fly you for £150 return, and the other (I forget which) would charge you £149.99. A nice, cosy setup at the expense of potential passengers.

This was before Ryanair revolutionised business air travel for small business people without expense accounts—*the* reason I won't hear a word against them. Within a few years, I was booking Ryanair flights for £25 one way, in the hope I'd have time to take them—and not worrying too much if I didn't.

So I booked with BA and flew to Paris one Friday in early 1986, booked into a hotel for the weekend, and waited for Monday, when the Rungis market would be open. I could save £500 by travelling out on Friday and back on Monday—though I had to spend three nights in a hotel, which, with meals and extras, probably cost more than the saving on the ticket.

However, it did allow me to wander the city and admire the wonderful architecture, which I'd always been smitten with. My only regret was not being able to take Jan, who needed to stay at home to deal with the fruit and veg, the riding holidays, and so on.

On Monday morning, I hadn't much time to spare. My return flight was at around 1 p.m., so I reckoned I would need to be away from the market by 10 a.m. at the latest.

I had done a recce on Sunday—gone out to Rungis (though I knew it was closed)—just to find exactly where the fish market was and how to get there with the least amount of wasted time.

My travel alarm woke me at 3 a.m., and I was on the move by 3:30, arriving at Rungis around 4. I wandered through the stands, making note of those that had winkles for sale. Not many had them, though every fish imaginable—from dozens of countries—could be found on one or another of the stalls.

At the stands that did have winkles, I lingered and examined them. Eventually, I was approached by a salesman—clearly hoping I was a buyer.

"Non, Monsieur, je suis un fournisseur des bigorneaux d'Écosse"—*No, sir, I am a supplier of winkles from Scotland.*

I asked if the winkles he had were from Scotland.

"Non, Monsieur, ils sont Irlandaise."

Would you be interested in winkles from Scotland? I asked, in my best O-Level French (failed).

"Attendez, Monsieur," *Wait, sir*, he said, disappearing through the back of the stall.

He reappeared with another guy—much better dressed—the kind of man you just know doesn't have to wash his hands before going home from work.

Not without some difficulties in understanding each other, I eventually gathered that his winkles came from a firm in the French Basque Country called Moulexport, who apparently imported them from Ireland.

At first, I couldn't understand what he was talking about, but he kept asking if the winkles were what sounded like *"grampay."*

Eventually, by trial and error—and with some assistance from one of the upstairs office girls who had a smattering of English—I understood that *"grampay"* was actually *grimpe'*, the French word for *climbing*. It described a process whereby the winkles had climbed up a board before coming to market.

It was actually a legal requirement in France that winkles were made *grimpe'* before being sold to the public. The process involved placing the winkles in a tank, filling it with seawater, and then inserting flat boards vertically for the winkles to crawl up—thus making them *grimpe'* (i.e., *climbed*) before putting them in boxes or bags for public sale.

Any that didn't crawl up the boards after a day or so were assumed to be dead and thrown out.

They weren't always dead—sometimes they were just *fatiguée*, i.e., too tired to crawl—but the beauty of the process was that all

16

those which had crawled up the boards were demonstrably alive and therefore unlikely to poison anyone.

All of this was not only news to me—it was also food for thought on the flight home.

I didn't have the facilities to make my winkles *grimpe'*, so I would have to abandon any ideas of selling directly to Paris. However, I had taken the contact details for Moulexport, who were located in Hendaye, in the Basque Country, just by the Spanish border.

Chapter 3

Back home, I had plenty to think about but also plenty to do with the fruit and veg still continuing, as were the riding holidays. But my eyes were now firmly fixed on a different future, one I felt to be just out of reach, yet definitely achievable.

Before that could happen, though, I knew I would need to get more winkles than I would ever find on Arran. And before that, there were a few bureaucratic hoops to jump through.

The First Challenge: Transport

If I was going to buy more winkles, I would need a bigger truck than the 35 cwt Fiat van I had recently bought for the fruit and veg, which could only legally carry just over one ton of winkles.

That created another problem.

The next size up from 35 cwt was seven and a half tons. But at that size, I needed a Goods Vehicle Operator's Licence. That was fairly straightforward, as long as I was only carrying my own goods—which, at that stage, I was. So I applied for and received the (Restricted) Operator's Licence, then started looking for a suitable vehicle to buy and register on the licence.

Eventually, I found a 7.5-ton Dodge "curtainsider" costing £4,500, which would be legal for carrying four tons of winkles.

In the UK, commercial vehicles are designated by their **Gross Vehicle Weight** (GVW)—the maximum allowed total weight of the vehicle and its cargo. It's rigorously policed, with random checks on motorways and main A roads, and there are stiff fines and penalty points on your operator's licence for transgressions.

So, a 7.5-ton curtain-sided truck typically weighs around 3½ tons when empty and is not permitted to exceed 7.5 tons fully loaded. That meant I could legally carry around four tons of winkles—provided the total didn't go over the GVW.

Finding the Pickers

With transport sorted, I spent a lot of time and effort (still pre-internet) tracking down local newspapers along the UK coast—from Wick to Hull on the east coast and from Stornoway to North Wales on the west.

I placed adverts in as many papers as I could find:

"WINKLES WANTED – Best prices paid. Regular collection. Call [number]."

Then I waited for responses—which, in time, began to come in.

The main issue with those responses was their scattered distribution—and the small quantities involved, which in many cases would make collection uneconomic.

What I really needed were replies from men who were already buying from other pickers, had a decent quantity to sell, and were just looking for a better price or a more reliable buyer.

Sifting through the replies to find *those* people wasn't easy. Human nature being what it is, there was a natural tendency to exaggerate the quantity—and quality—of what they had to sell.

But after a couple of weeks, I could see a pattern forming. There was a realistic chance I'd be able to make economically sensible collections.

Autumn/Winter 1986

I discovered there was a merchant in Lochaber named Rodney George, who dealt with Spain, where prices were apparently better. So I got his number, gave him a call, and told him I could supply around one ton per week.

I was surprised when he asked, "How many of the Arran winkles are in a kilo?"

I had no idea.

"Why do you want to know?" I asked.

"Well," he said, "it gives me an idea of their size."

Of course—it was obvious once explained. The fewer winkles in a kilo, the larger they tend to be.

"I'll go and do that now and call you back," I told him.

I measured out a couple of handfuls, weighed exactly one kilo using Jan's good kitchen scales (to her considerable dismay), and then sat down to count.

Jan thought I'd completely lost the plot.

But once I had the number, I phoned Rodney back and gave him the count.

"Well, if they're all like that," he said, "I can pay *this* much per kilo."

The price he quoted was about 50% higher than what Primel was paying.

I told him I'd get back to him in a couple of weeks.

With that figure in mind, I worked out a price I could afford to offer the local dealers, and over the next week, I went to see them all.

These were meetings I wasn't looking forward to.

Though my proposition made sense to me, I had no idea how they'd respond. If even one of them refused and preferred to continue with their existing arrangements, I'd have to rethink my entire strategy.

But I needn't have worried.

All three were businesslike and saw the value of working together rather than against each other. It made sense—for all of us.

Later that week, I called Rodney back and arranged to sell him around two tons of winkles. He wanted me to take them to Tarbet, by Loch Lomond, to meet a Spanish truck.

Over the weekend, I gathered winkles from the other dealers and the Merkland travellers using the Iveco 35 cwt van. On Tuesday morning, I caught the boat to Ardrossan and set off for Tarbet.

Rodney had told me to be there for 1 p.m., so I arrived in plenty of time... and waited. And waited.

And waited.

Finally, around 4 p.m., the Spanish truck appeared. I got tipped and was soon on my way to Glasgow, where I was staying the night before heading to the fruit market in the morning.

I was to learn that rendezvous with Spanish trucks **always** involved a lot of waiting.

Everything about meeting them seemed to be chaotic—mostly because they had to tip their own loads of fruit and veg at markets at times they couldn't control.

It was a problem I would eventually encounter for myself—though, at that time, I had no idea that was in my future.

Indeed, it was realising just how chaotic it all was that eventually gave me the confidence to look beyond selling to other Scottish merchants, to the possibility of selling and delivering to the people they were dealing with—reasoning that someone as well-organised as I liked to think I was could do it at least as well, if not better.

But all that would come later and wasn't even in my thoughts at that point.

For the moment, I just wanted to consolidate the buying setup I had put in place and learn a bit more about the business I was now involved in.

Adverts

The replies to the adverts were rolling in now, and I felt able to sketch out rounds that seemed viable.

I'd had very promising responses from Fife, Dundee, and Montrose, which could all be done together. Also, Berwick-on-Tweed, Hartlepool, Scarborough, and Whitby, which would mean quite a long trip but could be combined with picking up from a couple of promising-sounding folk down the A74.

There was also a merchant from North Wales—Keith Ross—who was prepared to meet me around Carlisle or Penrith with around a ton.

All in all, by November, I reckoned I could pick up around 3 or 4 tons from the A74/North East England run, and about the same from the East Coast of Scotland run.

I had also been contacted by some folk in the Western Isles in the broadest sense, including Skye and Mull, but as that was Rodney's home territory, I decided to pass on them for the meantime.

As 1986 drew to a close, I learned for the first time about the importance of Christmas to the shellfish industry—and winkles in particular.

The demand is so great at that time that I came to think of the month of December as *the fifth quarter of the year.*

I had spent most of the month driving around Scotland and the North of England buying winkles and answering calls from people wanting to buy them. I had maxed out all my credit cards in the process while pushing my overdraft to its limit.

I can remember exactly the moment I felt sure our financial future was secure.

It was **23 December 1986**.

I had just returned home from a trip taking in Fife, Dundee, Montrose, Edinburgh, Berwick, Scarborough, and Whitby with a full load of winkles, delivered them in Glasgow, and caught the six o'clock boat home for Christmas.

At home were messages from buyers and sellers of winkles wanting to do more business—which meant I would need to be off on the first boat I could get after Christmas Day.

But I'm getting a bit ahead of myself, there were still a few matters to be attended to.

Chapter 4:

Health Certs

Another bureaucratic hurdle lay in the paperwork required to export any shellfish to Europe. When selling to Primel or Rodney, they had taken care of all that side of it.

This was pre-Single Market, and the drill for France was that you needed to have a customs agent in the UK to handle the export process and liaise with a French agent who would deal with the import side.

Once you had found all this out and made some enquiries, there was nothing difficult about the process. But there was potentially one major problem with the required paperwork: the Health Certificate.

A **Live Bivalve Mollusc Health Certificate** (H/C) was required to accompany each consignment of winkles, which could be obtained from the Local Authority—in our case, Cunninghame District Council (CDC).

The need for this particular H/C came about essentially because of a bureaucratic cock-up, which would come to have greater salience in future years. When drawing up the rules governing the export of shellfish, the UK authorities had included winkles—which are gastropods—with bivalve molluscs (oysters, mussels, cockles, etc.).

Bivalves are filter feeders and prone to making people ill if they come from unclean waters and haven't been purified. But gastropods are different. They live on algae and seaweed and, thanks to one of nature's symmetries, are idiot-proof in terms of safety to eat.

The winkle is attached to its shell by a membrane. The cooking necessary to detach that membrane is precisely the amount of cooking required to kill any harmful bacteria in the flesh—making boiled winkles the safest of all small shellfish to eat.

Once we had the H/C—after some to-ing and fro-ing around quantities and provenance—we had the certificate we needed.

But before I could set my plans in motion, there was one more problem needing attention: **money**.

Up until this point, I had been financing my buying by maxing out my two credit cards—both with limits of £5,000—and always careful to pay them back before any interest was added.

All the potential suppliers were going to want to be paid in cash when I picked up their winkles, and some of the potential customers weren't expecting to pay until four weeks after delivery—at the earliest. That was going to require quite a lot of hard cash and understanding on the part of the Bank of Scotland.

Winkles at that time were costing, on average, £400–500 per ton. So to meet my target of five tons per week meant I would need around £2,000–2,500 each week for winkles alone—never mind all the other costs involved in running the business. At least £3,000 per week for a month or more before I got paid for any of my sales.

I was already overdrawn to the max with the bank, so I had to work up a cash flow projection for the next three months to show they'd get their money back—plus interest—to convince them to finance me.

Of course, they wanted every asset I owned as security, as banks do. But that was part of the price of being in the game.

I was quite relaxed about it—probably more relaxed than I should have been in the circumstances. Though I was increasingly confident that the tide in my affairs, in Shakespeare's phrase, was coming to the flood—and I didn't intend to miss that tide.

And so, on **17 November 1986**, having drawn £5,000 in cash from the bank and worked out a schedule, I set off.

My route would take me to Ardrossan, then Kilmarnock to pick up some wooden pallets I would need, then down the A74 to meet Arthur Kenny—a merchant from Kirkcudbright—at a café on that road. Then on to Penrith and another café to meet Keith Ross. Next, over the A66 to Scotch Corner to meet some lads from Hartlepool and some more from Whitby, finally turning round and heading back the way I'd come, with over four tons of winkles aboard.

That night, I slept in the cab of the truck in a layby off the A74—and damned cold it was too. But although tired and cold, I was happy. The day had gone better than I could have hoped for, and I felt energised and ready to go again as soon as my compulsory driver's rest period was up.

I had arranged storage for the winkles at a depot in Glasgow, so I put them in there and then set off along the M8, headed for the East Coast.

Having done deliveries of fruit and veg at home to hotels, shops, and restaurants for a few years, I was quite good at estimating how long a stop would take and how long it would take to get from A to B—always allowing some extra time for slippage in the schedule, which was always liable to happen.

This was important in several ways.

To me personally, because I hate being late. I also hate letting people down—so if I said I'd be in Dundee at 2 p.m., I needed to be in Dundee at 2 p.m.

But it was also important to my suppliers. Quite a few of them had been accustomed to being kept waiting—often for hours—by the people coming to buy their winkles, and they appreciated being shown that consideration.

For me, it was also about **respect**.

They were the ones doing the hard graft of picking the winkles. As pickers, they were often accused of being skivers—though no skiver would last very long out at the crack of dawn in all weathers picking wilks.

As long as they were putting money in my pocket, I felt the very least they deserved was my respect—and they had it.

They also had better prices than they had been accustomed to—which, in the end, was the main reason they were selling to me.

Another barb often aimed at wilk pickers was "Oh, they're all on benefits." Some probably were, though many were not, and picked wilks to supplement their income from other employment. Particularly in the Highlands and Islands, many pickers were small farmers and crofters—some of the hardest working and most independent-minded people in the country.

Being a wilk picker meant you were your own boss. You worked when you wanted to and stayed at home when you didn't, and nobody would get on your case if you did that. There was no boss berating you the next time you went to work. Then, when it came to selling your catch, you could choose to sell to whoever gave you the best deal—and part of the deal was not messing you about or keeping you waiting in a car park or layby for hours on end.

My schedule that day was Glenrothes, Dundee, then Montrose, then back to Drummond's storage depot in Glasgow on Yorkhill Quay, with another two and a half tons on board.

Another night spent sleeping in the cab of the truck. Then, in the morning, I got all the winkles out on the concrete outside the depot and made them up on pallets, ready for Rodney's truck to pick them up.

Finally, I went into the fruit market to buy the fruit I needed for the fruit and veg round at home, then back to Ardrossan and home on the last boat of the day.

Arran folk generally don't talk about "the ferry" or "ferries"— it's always just "the boat," which is (or was before the current ferries shambles began) universally understood to refer to the Ardrossan–Brodick ferry. That route has lately become the Troon–Brodick ferry.

Frequently, we'll dispense with "the boat" altogether and simply say "the three-fifteen" or "the six o'clock"—the well-known historic sailing times. Though with all the well-documented ferry fiascos recently, everything has changed. Hardly anybody has a clue about boat times now, or even which mainland port the boat will sail from—or even if it will sail at all.

When referring to the Lochranza–Claonaig ferry, on the other hand, that would be "the Lochranza boat," or simply "the wee boat." It's our true lifeline boat—the only one we've been able to rely on lately in almost all weathers.

A couple of years ago, Jan and I had left our youngest daughter Lauren at Glasgow Airport for a flight to Bangkok. We left the airport around 2 p.m. after Lauren had gone through security, intending to catch the 3:20 boat from Ardrossan on which we were booked, which would have got us home around 5 p.m.

Around 2:30 we discovered that the boat had broken down and there would be no further sailings to or from Brodick that day. So we booked into a hotel, planning to get the first boat in the morning.

In the early evening we discovered that it was thought unlikely that the Ardrossan–Brodick service would resume before the following afternoon, at the earliest. So we decided to make the three-hour drive to Tarbert through the night (in winter the Claonaig boat sails from Tarbert), in hopes of catching the first boat from there around 7 a.m.

We caught that boat, but nevertheless, Lauren had arrived in Bangkok before we arrived home.

I worked away like that through the winter of 1986 and spring of 1987, picking up one or two small French and Spanish customers along the way. They sent their own trucks to Scotland—usually for other shellfish like crab and lobster—in trucks specially adapted for that purpose, with aerated tanks full of seawater, known as vivier trucks. These also carried winkles, usually in the passage between the tanks in the middle of the truck.

I was operating a Volvo F6 truck at that point, which could carry 8 to 9 tons legally. That was all I then needed—though if my plans came to fruition, it soon wouldn't be.

31

International Operator's Licence

To operate a Heavy Goods Vehicle (HGV) over 7.5 tons on European roads at that time, you had to have a licence known as an **International Operator's Licence**. Someone in the company had to be the designated **Transport Manager**, responsible for all the various legal issues such as vehicle roadworthiness, valid road licences, and checking the drivers' hours.

To become a Transport Manager, you had to take a course, learn all the necessary details, and then sit an exam. If you passed, you were awarded something called a CPC.

I hadn't the time to do this—and, to be honest, as someone for whom the day I left school had been one of the happiest of my life, I hadn't much inclination either.

So Jan volunteered to do it—and passed first time—to become the Transport Manager for Sandy MacAlister Shellfish.

In March, I took the HGV Class 1 test to enable me to drive any size of truck.

Since there were a lot of winkle pickers in "the Three Toons" (as Ardrossan, Saltcoats, and Stevenston are known), I had rented a small yard in Saltcoats where we were buying, grading, and sorting winkles.

This meant I needed to employ people to do that, as I couldn't be there every day, and pickers wanted to bring their catch and get paid for it daily. This yard was no more than adequate for the job and had no parking—which made it unsuitable as an HGV Operating Centre, a wee problem.

I converted a potato grader to take winkles, installed it in the yard, and started buying winkles there—mainly at first from a squad of pickers from the Three Toons, whom I had got to know when they had sold me winkles picked on trips to Arran. Some of them eventually became the first employees of the business.

Finally, we were good to go.

So I contacted Monsieur Taffard, the manager of Moulexport, and arranged to visit him in Hendaye to discuss a deal for him to buy my winkles.

And so I flew from Gatwick to Bilbao on the 22nd of May 1987, after driving there in the F6 and having an argument with the parking people about whether I could use their car park. I could—after a twenty-minute stand-off only resolved by a manager—and was met at the airport by Pierre, one of Moulexport's employees, who spoke about as much English as I did French and with whom I would be staying that night before going to meet Monsieur Taffard in the morning.

As luck would have it, the next day, early in the morning in New Zealand, Scotland were playing France in the Rugby World Cup, kicking off about 4 a.m. French time. Rugby is big in the French Basque Country, so Pierre and his father were intending to watch the game and invited me to join them. Honour was shared as the match ended in a 20–20 draw, and after some breakfast, we headed for Moulexport's premises in Hendaye.

Monsieur Taffard, a short, fairly round man, showed me around his yard, which was fairly new and well equipped, and explained how he paid for imported shellfish such as winkles and mussels he imported by the lorry load from Spain—by Bill of Exchange. When he received the winkles, he would write me a Bill of Exchange for the value of the invoice, which I could take to my bank, whose international division would send it to a French bank with whom they had a relationship. They would pay the international division of my bank in French francs (this was before the Euro and the internet). My bank would then convert the francs to sterling and credit my account accordingly.

So on that basis, we made a deal for me to deliver a load of winkles within the next few weeks at a price we were both happy with, and I flew back to Gatwick later that day, raring to get started.

My confidence had been boosted by seeing the Irish winkles in Moulexport's yard. They were quite small and in 50-kilo hessian sacks, which the staff hated having to handle. I knew we could do better. Our sizes were better, and we packed everything in 25-kilo nets.

Never forget the guys doing the heavy lifting at the other end. If your product is easier for them to handle than that of your competitors, that could just be the factor which tips the balance in your favour—if everything else is equal and their boss is sick of them moaning about the extra work or harder work dealing with your opposition's product.

So, on the 18th of June 1987, with a ton of winkles from the island on board, I caught the 8:20 boat and headed off to Fife and Dundee after stopping at the yard at Saltcoats and Drummond's depot in Glasgow to pick up some winkles from the North. That night, I slept in the cab in Dundee, ready to set off as early as possible the next day.

By that night, I was in Manchester with a full load of winkles after picking up more down the A74. I had a booking on the Saturday night ferry from Portsmouth to St Malo, so I needed to be in Portsmouth by 8 p.m. I made another early start on Saturday morning and was at Portsmouth Harbour in plenty of time to do the paperwork and check in for the 21:30 sailing.

After a decent sleep in a cabin on the ferry, I drove onto the quay at St Malo at 7 a.m. French time. But then I had a wait of around an hour, as it was Sunday, for the vet to check the load and take a sample. It was all basically a formality before I could get on the road—which I was both eager to do and apprehensive about, as I had never driven in France, or on the right, before.

This was in the days before the internet and sat-navs, so I had my road atlas of France spread out to my left as I followed the "Toutes Directions" signs heading for the dual carriageway Route National 137 and the town of Rennes, my first target en route. From Rennes, the N137 continued towards Nantes, and I was enjoying the feeling of exhilaration, doing what I had been aiming towards since starting the business.

The sun was shining, the roads were quiet, the fields were full of sunflowers and beautiful, weed-free crops of barley and wheat, which the farmer in me couldn't help but admire, and everything seemed right with the world. I had been a bit worried about negotiating Nantes, which is a sizeable city, but I needn't have worried. Even then, Nantes had its own peripherique (ring road), well signposted and also quiet, with it being Sunday.

From Nantes, I headed towards Parthenay with the intention of picking up the A10 motorway to Bordeaux at Poitiers, which I did in the early afternoon. By evening, I was through Bordeaux—another easily negotiated city with a peripherique—and spent the night at Cestas services just south of Bordeaux.

Another night sleeping in the cab, then an early start after a breakfast of hard-boiled eggs, bread, coffee, and croissants, and an uneventful drive down past Bayonne and Biarritz, arriving at Moulexport in the early afternoon.

When the Moulexport staff started to unload the winkles, I jumped up in the truck to help and received my first lesson in the different treatment of truck drivers on the continent compared to the UK. They insisted I stay on the ground while they got on with the tipping.

Truckers don't talk about unloading—even though you will almost always unload with a pallet barrow and a forklift or by hand (handballing), it is usually referred to as tipping or getting tipped.

Their view, common everywhere I subsequently went in Europe, was that my job was over. I'd driven the truck and brought the load to them. It was their job to deal with the load. I wasn't complaining and enjoyed a cup or two of coffee while sorting out the paperwork, including the all-important bill of exchange—the payment for the winkles.

I had still not sorted out a back load, so around five o'clock, after the fridge had been washed out, I set off heading back home and parked up again at Cestas that evening. That night, I allowed myself the luxury of a bed in the Hotel Campanile, located within the service area.

A couple of days later, I was back home in Arran with a real feeling of "job done." But of course, it was only half a job. I still had to find back loads, and for that, I knew I needed a bigger truck to make the transport side of the operation profitable in its own right.

Chapter 5

I should say a word here about the fruit and vegetable business. One local wiseacre thought it necessary, around this time, to tell my daughter, aged nine, that her father, although he always seemed very busy, never stuck at anything for very long. One minute it was cattle and sheep, the next it was horses, then it was vegetables and now it was wilks. What would it be next? he wondered.

I was, and remain, proud of the quality of the vegetables we grew. Growing several acres each year, for a few years we supplied the island with vegetables of a quality, variety and quantity never previously known on Arran. Our broccoli, cauliflower, cabbages, Brussels sprouts, courgettes and leeks were the equal of any in the country.

As previously related, the vegetables were profitable and the venture ended only because the potential returns, relative to the work involved, in growing and supplying vegetables to the Isle of Arran (population 4,500 approx.) failed to match the potential returns, relative to the work involved, in buying and supplying winkles to Holland, France and Spain (population 134 million approx.). And as previously related, being stretched as a family beyond any sensible limits, we couldn't do both. Stopping the vegetables and concentrating on the winkles was the proverbial no-brainer.

My next task, in between buying and selling and making three more trips to Moulexport in the next six weeks, was to find a more suitable truck. Finally, after looking at a few which I felt were unsuitable for one reason or another, in mid-August I went to see a second-hand Volvo F7 eight-wheeler (four-axle truck) which could legally carry a fifteen-ton payload with a fridge body and—luxury— a sleeper cab with a night heater, at the Scania dealers in Renfrew.

They had taken it in part exchange and were not too difficult to deal with. Even so, I was committing myself to paying back around £1,000 per month for the next two and a half years, on top of everything else, so I needed another trip to see Jim Hill at the bank with an explanation of how it was all going to work out. Fortunately, he could see the upside and was happy to back me.

Some people referred to their bank manager as God. I saw them rather as more like the Pope—God's representative on Earth. It was necessary to remember that they had people to answer to too, like area managers etc., and if they couldn't explain why an account was causing the bank a problem, their neck was on the line, which meant their trust in you and readiness to lend to you would be damaged.

My philosophy in dealing with the bank was never to promise anything I wasn't sure I could do, and if anything unexpected happened to put that in doubt, to get straight on to the manager and explain what had happened, what the likely consequences were, and how I planned to deal with it.

I can honestly say, from the day I started the shellfish business until the day I retired, I never had a problem with the Bank of Scotland (BOS) in Brodick. Jim Hill and those who came after him were as good as gold with me.

However, I do still have in my possession a letter from a previous manager, from before I'd started the shellfish business, when I was farming and trying to get the vegetable business going, telling me—and I quote—"Our Head Office are not convinced this latest venture will succeed, however they are prepared to give you an opportunity to reduce dependence on bank borrowing, failing which a sale of assets will be insisted upon."

The potential consequences of incurring the displeasure of "Our Head Office" were never far from my mind for many years, especially so during a period when bad debts were a constant problem, though that was a few years in the future and there was an unexpected postscript which, at the time of receiving that letter, would have been unthinkable.

I had also now rented premises in Tain, north of Inverness, and we were now having winkles arrive from all over Scotland, plus some from England, Wales and Northern Ireland, with more suppliers wanting to sell to us. I had sourced some potential new customers in France and Spain, and the turnover of the business, which had escalated fast, was on course to more than double.

It meant another visit to the BOS was required, and another hike in our overdraft limit was negotiated.

But I still needed to find back loads to pay for the return journey after tipping the winkles. I had got in contact with a guy called David Peake, in Valencia in the south of Spain. He had worked for the Ford Motor Company in Dagenham before being moved out to their operation in Valencia, where he had worked for a time before leaving and setting up his own business as a broker, dealing in fruit and veg like onions, oranges, tomatoes etc.—all the stuff which was coming into the UK from Spain in ever-increasing volume at that time.

He said he could get me full loads of onions and oranges if I had markets for them.

David was an interesting guy who amazed me one day when he said that for motor manufacturers, making cars was nothing more than a means of generating cash flow for their financial people to make money on the foreign exchange markets, which was where most of their profits were actually made.

I had been buying most of my fruit and veg from Tony Brogan in the Glasgow fruit market, so I approached him first with the question, "Would he be interested in full loads of onions or oranges from Valencia?"

The onion season was just getting going, so he was quite keen and we agreed a price and approximate date for delivery. So I was now all set and made preparations for my first trip to Spain after I had tipped the next load of winkles at Moulexport. But the quantities of winkles we were now getting were more than they could handle, and I had been looking around for new customers, as relations with Rodney were becoming a bit fraught, as we were now being frequently contacted by suppliers in "his" area of the country, on the lookout for a better deal.

Gradually, the customer list increased and, as the new customers were all in or close to Normandy—at Cherbourg, Granville, Cancale and St Malo—I could drop off their winkles on the way to Moulexport without losing much time, while using the cheapest crossing from Portsmouth to Cherbourg in Normandy.

At this time, my life was dominated by the round trips: Arran–Saltcoats–Fife–Dundee–Tain–Glasgow–Portsmouth–Cherbourg–Hendaye, tip and return. But the return trip empty was uneconomic, so on 21 August 1987, with some trepidation, I crossed the border into Spain for the first time, en route to Valencia for my first load of onions.

Recently (April 2024), Jan and I made the same journey by car, from the border at Hendaye to Valencia via Pamplona, Zaragoza and Teruel—motorway or dual carriageway all the way. But in 1987, it was very different.

The first part from Irun to Pamplona was up a steeply winding road in the direction of Santesteban, one of those Spanish roads with three lanes, where the middle lane is for overtaking only by the traffic going uphill. As I had tipped in France and was empty, I could use that lane, passing other trucks which were crawling up the hill fully loaded.

Pamplona, which had no ring road and only tiny direction signs in the town which, if you blinked, you could miss, had to be negotiated by way of the same streets in which they run the bulls during their famous Fiesta.

From Pamplona to Zaragoza was a relief—motorway or dual carriageway all the way—but after Zaragoza, it was back to a three-lane highway most of the way to Valencia, with one particularly notorious stretch of around 30 kilometres from Calamocha to Daroca, which appeared to be cobbled in the way the truck bounced as it went over it, such that by Daroca, I felt physically sick.

Again, as a farmer, the terrain and crops—or lack of them—was interesting, with the main livestock farming appearing to be pig farming, with many small piggeries and some poultry houses dotting what looked like a pretty barren landscape.

By evening I was at Valencia, where, according to the directions David had given me, there was no alternative to going through the middle of the city to reach the packing house with the onions, on the far side. However, I negotiated it successfully, much to my relief, and met the boss there, who told me they would be packing and loading the onions in the morning. I would be on my way by lunchtime tomorrow.

That night in Valencia, the temperature must have been around 25 degrees Celsius and the cab was stifling hot as I got my head down. I opened a window just an inch or so and slept without a shirt on. Big mistake.

In the morning I got up, watched the staff packing the onions, palletising them and loading the pallets in the back of the F7. Meanwhile, I was having some trouble understanding what I was being told by the extremely efficient secretary, the boss's daughter, Maria. In every Spanish office, there always seems to be a Maria, if not several. She kept saying I had to go to visit what sounded like Celia, which was the first I had heard of Celia.

So I phoned David Peake, who said what she meant was that I would have to do "the revision", basically a quality inspection of the onions at a government station at the small town of Silla, about ten kilometres south of Valencia. I was used to having veterinary inspections of the winkles coming into the country but wasn't expecting the same thing on the way out. It wasn't a problem, more an inconvenience, when I had expected to be turned around and heading for home in the early afternoon. To make things worse, I learned I would probably miss the morning revision and have to hang about till the late afternoon.

The Inspectors' way of working was a classic of its type. I arrived at the station at Silla, which, to be fair, was well signposted, at around 3 p.m. Several other UK trucks were there, and one of the drivers told me nothing would happen until after 4:30 p.m.

Around 4, there was a bit of a kerfuffle and two or three official-looking guys came out of what was obviously the office. I thought, great, here we go. But no. They had only come out to have a smoke while they finished their lunchtime coffee, and when they had done that, they disappeared back inside.

Sometime between 4:30 and 5:00, they reappeared, and this time they meant business. Within about half an hour, they had opened the back doors of all the trucks there, by now around twenty, helped themselves to handfuls of the tomatoes, cucumbers, strawberries and so on in some of the trucks, stamped our papers, and we could all be on our way.

I put it down to the universal Spanish practice of shutting up shop for lunch from 2 p.m. to 4:30 p.m., but one of the other drivers told me, and I subsequently saw for myself, it was exactly the same at the morning revision. No matter how early you arrived, nothing would happen until around 1 p.m., then there would be a flurry of activity and it would all be done and dusted by 2, when they would stop for lunch until 4:30.

Finally released from the compound at Silla, I negotiated the city but was becoming increasingly concerned by the itchiness I was feeling on my back. My stupidity in opening a window the previous evening had left me with umpteen mosquito bites and no way of doing anything about it other than to wriggle around on my seat trying to scratch them on the back of it. This was a situation I had to put up with until I was almost back home.

I had decided not to return the way I had come through Spain, but rather to take the motorway up the coast past Barcelona, crossing the border at La Jonquera, then Perpignan, Narbonne, Toulouse and

Bordeaux. At that point, I would retrace my steps along the same route I had taken from Cherbourg.

Two days later, I was back at the top of the hill above Cherbourg, the only place in France my phone worked, and learned that because of heavy tourist traffic, that night's Portsmouth boat was full. I had the choice of sailing to Weymouth that night or waiting until the next morning if I wanted Portsmouth. It was a clear decision. I had been away for nine days, I still wouldn't be home for another two at best, and I would be starting to do it all over again in three, or at most four, days.

The following evening I was back in Glasgow and tipped the onions at Brogan's early the next morning, in time to get the 12:30 boat home.

That was how it continued through the rest of the autumn, winter, and spring of 1987 to 1988. My operating centre was at home on Arran, and I had to bring the truck back there regularly to be compliant with the regulations. On occasion, I could leave it at Tom Frew's farm at Stevenston, and I would do a round trip every fortnight buying onions or oranges in Spain and selling them in Glasgow to Brogan's, or sometimes to fruit and veg merchants in Birmingham and Manchester markets.

I spent the night of the Great Storm of October 1987 at Scotch Corner at the junction of the A1 and A66 after loading a ton of winkles from the lads from Hartlepool, and never noticed a thing until I heard them talking about it on the radio in the morning.

As 1988 went on, the winkles we were getting kept increasing, and it became imperative to find new customers. At that point, my fortnightly fifteen-ton load would be around ten or twelve for Moulexport and the rest for the smaller customers down the Cotentin Peninsula.

The balance we were selling to French and Spanish customers who sent their own trucks to Scotland, usually for crab and lobster and so on—companies like Cetarea El Rinconín from Gijón in Asturias, Thaëron Frères from South Brittany, and one or two random others.

Chapter 6

S ometime in the summer of 1988, I was contacted by a shellfish merchant from Oviedo in Asturias, Enrique Garcia, who phoned up out of the blue one day, announced he was in Scotland, and asked if he could come to see me to talk about winkles. I said yes, and he appeared the next day. He was very plausible, said he was sourcing all kinds of shellfish and wanted to go all round the country meeting suppliers of all kinds of fish and shellfish, but for some reason to do with his driving licence, he was unable to rent a car. He wanted five tons of winkles per week and asked if I could drive him round the country. Foolishly, I agreed, and the next day we set off. Jan came too and did most of the driving for the next two days round the north of Scotland, before we deposited him back at Glasgow Airport, with an agreement to bring him five tons of winkles on my next trip.

The first shipment to Garcia went okay, no problems, but the second one brought a major headache. A couple of days after I got home from that trip, Garcia came on the phone. He wanted a reduction, a credit, on the invoice for that shipment. They were all too small and some of them were dead, he claimed. I told him there may have been a few smaller winkles in the shipment, but not many, and categorically there were no dead winkles—none. I also reminded him that his brother had helped me unload them and had not made any complaint at the time, though the fact that the shed he had put them in had no refrigeration couldn't have helped. But he was adamant. He wasn't paying without a credit for half the cost of the shipment, which I had no intention of giving him. So there it rested, for months, although there was a postscript much later.

Claims for credits were the bane of my life, though that was only because I hadn't yet met credit's ugly sister—bad debt. If I had known at that point that within a few years I would have accumulated over a quarter of a million pounds of bad debt, I would probably have abandoned the business there and then.

With shellfish, which are a fragile commodity with sizes that are often different depending on who is judging them, there will always be losses and arguments about size and quality when they have to travel over long distances under refrigeration, often taking several days to make the journey. And that's before you factor bad actors into the equation.

By bad actors, I mean people who have no intention of paying their bills or are constantly claiming credits, who have no qualms about ripping you off and consider it a normal part of doing business. For example, there was one French company we dealt with who sent around their own truck. My last dealings with them came after they phoned up and said they were not paying for a couple of tons they'd picked up because the bags were light and had maggots in them. As chance would have it, I had been in our yard at Saltcoats when their truck had arrived and had helped to handball the bags onto pallets, so I knew with absolute certainty that their claims were nonsense.

Because they were dealing with many different Scottish suppliers, it was quite possible they had got some bags with maggots from somebody, which their driver hadn't noticed when loading them. Either they didn't know who had supplied them, so were claiming against everybody who had winkles on the truck, or did know but were just claiming against everybody anyway. Or, and this was quite common, they had had a bad losing week, for one reason or another, so had decided to claim against every single supplier of everything with some excuse, no matter how spurious, in hopes of making up their loss on the week. Most would contest the claim, but enough wouldn't or would accept part of the claim to at least mitigate their losses on the week.

Then there are people who maybe mean to pay, but for one reason or another, find themselves under financial pressure and can't pay. Some of them will be honest about it and promise to pay when their financial situation improves, which of course often it never does, but others will invent claims about size or quality or mortality (of the product) in order to get out of paying.

Then there are the real bad actors—companies which are basically criminal organisations that happen to deal in fish and shellfish, set up with the intention of defrauding their suppliers right from the start. After a period of paying on time, they would suddenly increase their orders, take delivery, then disappear, a practice I believe is known as long firm fraud.

Worth a mention too are those companies which would always claim shortage of weight in the bags (when delivery was by a third party). What usually happened there was the members of their staff weighing the product at reception were helping themselves, unknown to their bosses, who were told that a shipment had arrived five or ten or twenty kilos light.

In later years, when we were selling live prawns and razor clams and transporting them by air freight, there could be genuine problems of mortality caused by inadequate refrigeration facilities at some airports, sometimes involving boxes sitting on the tarmac on hot days for hours at a time.

I could count on the fingers of one hand the times when I got a genuine claim for a credit, which wasn't transport related, which I wasn't half expecting. Occasionally, particularly with the razor clams, you knew that there could be a problem with a shipment, but you couldn't afford not to just send them and hope for the best. Though in those circumstances, you had to always be prepared to come and go on the invoice if the customer complained.

The razor clams, though, were far in the future.

Initially, I was apprehensive about driving on the right and often found myself boxed in, in the inside lane of motorways, particularly where traffic was heavy in the vicinity of cities like Bordeaux, with ring roads congested with commuter traffic mingling with through traffic to and from the A63, the main western route between France and Spain and Portugal.

An epiphany came one day around 9 a.m. on the Bordeaux ring road, a three-lane motorway. I was crawling along in heavy traffic in the inside lane, unable to get out, when I noticed an artic truck coming down a pretty steep on-ramp a wee bit up ahead. Forty-plus tons of Austrian articulated truck was heading straight for the inside lane and was clearly not going to be giving way to the cars in that lane, or anything else. Owing to the topography at that point, his truck could probably be seen from the vehicles in the inside lane for around half a mile before the slip road entrance. Everyone in the inside lane either slowed down or moved into the middle lane, and he had clear space in front of him to enter the motorway.

That's how you do it, I thought, and I never looked back after that.

Before you sit your HGV test, when you're doing your training, your instructor will tell you that you must never use the size of your truck to bully or intimidate other drivers, which is good advice. But sometimes, when you are surrounded by cars driven by people who by and large don't appreciate the difficulties experienced by HGV drivers—such as the lack of acceleration, the need to go down the gears when balked, particularly when it's completely unexpected, and the difficulty of then regaining momentum—the differences in braking distance for a truck compared to a car become very relevant. Especially in traffic, when you are keeping a safe distance behind a vehicle and some smart aleck decides to nip into that space.

For instance, that Austrian truck driver was coming down a steep on-ramp towards a carriageway and traffic that was going uphill— not a very steep hill, but a hill nevertheless—and was visible to the traffic on the motorway. If he had approached slowly, some might have moved over to let him in, but some definitely wouldn't have, so he would have been reduced to almost stopping before he got on. Then once he was on, until he regained momentum, he would have been more of a hazard than he was by making his intentions crystal clear for all to see and adapt to.

For forty years I've followed the "only a fool breaks the two-second rule" mantra when in heavy traffic. For anyone who's never heard of it, it refers to always keeping at least two seconds behind the vehicle in front. It keeps everyone safe—until the aforementioned smart aleck sees the space you're leaving and nips into it as he weaves his way through the traffic. If you're driving a car, that's not too much of a problem, but in a fully loaded truck it most certainly is.

The biggest hazard on the road in my opinion is the driver who goes to make a manoeuvre then changes his mind and does something else, totally unexpected. In that kind of traffic, where commuter and other local traffic is mixed with strangers passing through, you have to be assertive, though not aggressive, otherwise you will get into trouble sooner or later.

All the messiness with Garcia had brought us to the attention of another Asturias merchant, Dioni Otimende of Lurrietxaso SA. He had been buying winkles from Rodney but contacted me that year wanting to buy from us. At first, I was reluctant, not wanting to create a rift with Rodney, but we had been having problems with some of the French customers' payments being very late. And with the unpaid invoice to Garcia, I felt I had no choice, since Otimende was offering to pay immediately and his reputation was that he was as good as his word.

Also, I had been contacted by a Dutch customer of good repute, Kopek BV, who wanted large quantities of winkles and would also pay for them immediately. So, somewhat reluctantly, I stopped supplying Rodney and moved on, as we had to do if we were going to continue to grow the business.

Chapter 7

The reason I had been confident of the potential of the winkle business was that, of all the shellfish in Scottish waters, winkles had the best risk and reward profile by a distance. When they were freshly picked, provided they were bagged and put in a fridge right away, they would stay alive for up to five or six weeks, provided only that the bags were turned over once a week or so. The key conditions were refrigeration and plenty of air round about them, though it was also essential that they had not been mistreated before refrigerating them.

By comparison, most other shellfish would only keep for a few days or a week or so at most unless in aerated tanks and were comparatively expensive and consequently a greater financial loss if they died.

For a day or two after returning home from my trips to France and Spain, I was cursed with terrible headaches, which I blamed on the release of tension on being home and away from the stress of the trip. The stress was real. You were on your own for ten to twelve days, driving mostly on foreign roads, fair game for any French or Spanish copper or petty official if you screwed up in any way, subject to umpteen different regulations concerning hours of driving, health of your load, maintenance of your truck, all of which, while perfectly right and proper, added to the pressure of trying to keep to a schedule with a perishable cargo aboard and occasional

55

breakdowns, knowing that any harm coming to your load would probably result in major financial loss.

This was long before the days of satnav or Google Maps. Usually, you had your road atlas open on the passenger seat, ready to be grabbed whenever you encountered a hurdle you had not anticipated or mentally noted when you had checked out the route ahead at your last stop.

For me, it was all about morale. Anything which damaged your morale was bad: encounters with traffic police, traffic jams, taking a wrong turn or going down an unsuitable road for an eight-wheel truck, having to go through the centre of cities like Granada with its warrens of narrow streets and barely visible road signs, arriving at a destination too late or too early to tip or load and losing time, bad weather, nights when the cab was too hot to sleep, nights when it was so hot you had to open a window knowing you could be eaten alive by mosquitos even though you had a fan running, nights when the cab heater was not working and it was too cold to sleep, having to park up for the night because of the drivers' hours regulations without enough food or water (and knowing it was your own fault because of poor planning—you knew you should have stopped at that last service station), breakdowns, and last but not least, effectively being not just away from home, but out of contact with home most of the time.

The mobile phone, a brick-like Motorola, one of the first on Arran, was an absolute boon while in the UK, even though using it in company—for instance, while travelling on the boat—caused a bit of embarrassment as some people seemed to think you were in some way showing off, as the early phones were horrendously expensive to buy and to use. But it was only a partial solution to the problem of keeping in touch, since in many parts of the country, including northern and western Scotland, the service was patchy at best and non-existent in many places, including in Europe.

On a good clear day, it worked at the top of the hill above Cherbourg, but that was all, and the rest of the time you were dependent on phone boxes, another source of stress.

Phone boxes? I can imagine younger people thinking, how could a phone box be stressful? But nobody living in the UK before mobile phones became ubiquitous will need to ask. If you could find one that had not been vandalised, it probably would not be working. If it was working, there would probably be a queue waiting to use it.

In France, phone boxes were a problem in a different way. Generally speaking, they were un-vandalised and worked pretty well. The problem was, going through the main street of multiple small towns, as the Route National 137 and other RN roads did in the days before the French motorway network was the pleasure to use it is today, phone boxes were usually situated at crossroads of the main road with other locally important roads. So, to use one, you had to first find a parking place, or more accurately, a place to stop. That could not be near the crossroads if you did not want to create a hazard, so you usually had to park at least a few hundred yards along the road and walk back, whatever the weather, preferably in the evening when it was quiet.

Small French towns were incredibly quiet in the evenings compared with similar sized UK towns at that time. What frequently happened was, I would do all this—sometimes in pouring rain—and phone home, only to get an engaged tone, which lasted for ten, fifteen, twenty minutes, sometimes even longer, by which time I felt I had to get back to the truck without having spoken to Jan, which was going to be the highlight of my day.

The problem was more often than not, one or other of our daughters calling or being called by their pals, totally oblivious.

We eventually solved that problem by having a second BT line installed which nobody was permitted to use or to even know the number, so it was always available for me to phone Jan whenever I had the chance.

Those were the things which were bad for morale, but what best boosted my morale can be summed up in one word: music.

I had a box of tapes which I had built up over the past few years of going about the country with fruit and veg and the beginnings of the winkle business. I had certain tapes which I invariably played in certain places and certain situations and to generate or get rid of certain moods. That, combined with a siege mentality—me against the world—was what got me through the difficult moments.

Developing a siege mentality while remaining positive, as you needed to be, was a tricky one. And those moments where negativity threatened needed to be dispelled as soon as possible. I found music to be the best solution.

When I left home going anywhere, in the truck, I usually kicked off with Dire Straits' *Walk of Life*, sometimes on repeat over and over, because I found it really upbeat and positive. If I was on my way eventually to the Continent, at the top of the String (the road between Shiskine and Brodick) I would usually go to Thin Lizzy's *Southbound*, for obvious reasons. It would usually get another airing as I left the M8 for the M74 and again when leaving Cherbourg for Southern France or Spain.

If I had to go through a city and down streets like in Valencia or Granada, it would be Tom Petty's *Runaway Trains* on repeat for its steady beat, which I found calming in a situation where calm watchfulness and a courteous manner was necessary. But if it was a city ring road like round Bordeaux or Paris, where everything was faster, more fluid with lots of lane changing and you needed all your wits about you plus a touch of assertiveness, it was usually the Rolling Stones' *The Last Time* or *It's All Over Now* or similar. Springsteen's *No Surrender* and Bob Seger's *Hollywood Nights* were good too.

Hitting the motorway out of Valencia or Granada, seeing those beautiful big blue Autopista signs (how I came to love those big blue signs after a few wrong turns on the outskirts of cities), which meant the end of congested city streets for a while and heading for home, was always John Denver's *Country Roads*, followed by *Mississippi*, which reminded me of home (Greenville), and would also get another airing about five minutes away from home. After getting off the boat at Brodick it had to be Dave Dudley's *Six Days on the Road*. One golden rule was that The Tourists' *So Good to Be Back Home Again* could not be played under any circumstances until half a mile from home, so the gods of trucking weren't displeased, but it would always be played from there till I switched off the engine.

There were plenty of other tapes in my box and all got a hearing over the couple of weeks or so I would be away, some more than others. Kenny Rogers and Dolly Parton's duet *Islands in the Stream* was a particular favourite, and all of the Eagles' canon, a lot of Tom Petty, Bryan Adams, Bob Seger and Springsteen, Bob Dylan and The Band, The Police, Rod Stewart, The Byrds and Billy Joel, and Simon and Garfunkel's greatest hits, plus too many country and western classics to mention.

The purpose of it all was to sustain my morale over the whole trip and I found it pretty effective. I never forgot to take my tapes on a trip, but I know if I had it would have been a much more miserable experience.

Essentially, the business, which I didn't yet know was going to dominate my life for the next thirty-five years, was built on the roads of Scotland, England, France and Spain, during those years between 1985 and 1990.

Travelling through France and Spain as a truck driver was an enlightening experience. You are always at a slight disadvantage in a right-hand drive vehicle when driving on the right, particularly when overtaking. I only had one scary moment because of that. On the road from Teruel to Valencia one morning, on a straight stretch of two-lane road just after Segorbe, I had been following a heavily loaded truck for miles, with no chance to pass it, when I spotted a clear stretch of road ahead as I squinted round the inside of the truck in front. I moved out to pass. As I was empty at this point, I gunned the F7, confident I had enough clear road before the next bend to easily pass the loaded truck.

But as I had moved out I had created a blind spot for myself which had prevented me spotting a small seven-and-a-half-ton type truck turning left out of a road at a right angle to the main road I was on. This truck was now on course to meet me head-on unless one of us did something about it, and the other guy had nowhere to go. His only option was to stop and hope I got back into my own lane before I hit him. I hit the brakes hard and just managed to get back in behind the truck I had been intent on passing, in time to avert a very nasty incident. I was a lot more cautious about passing anything on a two-lane road after that.

As a truck driver, I found that drivers generally treated you and your vehicle with a respect which I found almost entirely absent in later years when I made the same journeys in a car with a UK plate. When local drivers, particularly in France, are behind a car with a

UK plate, for some, it's like a red rag to a bull. Some almost have to get past you, as if it's their patriotic duty, no matter the circumstances or the danger to themselves or others.

I particularly remember one instance in the Vendée, of a Citroën overtaking Jan and me on a blind bend after being right up our backside for about half a mile or so and just avoiding, by inches, a car travelling in the opposite direction. What made it worse was that there were children in the back seat.

I also found the ordinary working person in both France and Spain to be much more pleasant when they could see that you were in their country for work rather than as a tourist, particularly if you made an effort to speak their language or respect their customs, like saying the ritual "Bonjour, Madame" or "Monsieur" when entering a shop, rather than, as you might in a strange town at home, just asking for what you want with few pleasantries.

I liked that aspect of French life, the ritual courtesies, though the handshaking of everyone you met in a workplace was a bit hard to get accustomed to—particularly if you had to do it all over again after lunch, as was the custom in some places.

It was a different life from the one I had known growing up on Arran in the 1950s, though with one definite echo—my liking, when I was a young boy, for spending my Saturdays travelling around the island on one of Bannatyne Motors' lorries with any driver I could persuade to take me, as they went about their deliveries to all parts of the island. That came to a sudden halt after an unfortunate incident concerning a runaway lorry and a cargo boat loaded with coal on Lamlash pier.

It's sometimes difficult to explain to young people just how different life in the Shiskine Valley was in the '50s. It was very much a farming community. Tourism was a relatively minor part of the economy by comparison with today. There were around thirty more or less full-time farming families, where today there are barely a third of that number.

There was very little "diversity" of the kind we know today. We were almost all straight, white Protestants, and the only diversity was between the two denominations of the Church of Scotland and the Free Church of Scotland. The most obvious differences were that the Church of Scotland sat down to pray but stood up to sing, with an organist to lead the singing, while the Free Church stood up to pray but sat down to sing, with someone called a "precentor" leading the music-free singing.

The first time I was aware of Roman Catholics was at the age of twelve in first year at the secondary school at Lamlash, when one of the teachers asked me to take a note to the headmaster's office, telling me not to look at it. I might not have thought of doing so otherwise, so of course I did—and it named all the class and their religion, including two boys from Brodick who were Catholics, much to my surprise, as it had never occurred to me that they were any different from the rest of us. Of course, they weren't, and I don't think most of we children had even heard of any non-Christian religions.

Most people in the valley attended one church or the other, though it would be wrong to characterise us as a religiously minded community. The most obvious manifestation of religiosity was the universal prohibition on doing anything that wasn't strictly necessary on Sundays, which were supposed to be days of rest. Permitted exceptions were, for example, milking dairy cows or any other welfare issue relating to livestock, such as calving or lambing, and of course checking their health.

I can still remember getting a new bike for my eighth birthday, which happened to fall on a Sunday, and setting off on it to show it to my uncle, who farmed about three quarters of a mile away. About a couple of hundred yards away from his house I met him out checking on some young cattle he had in a field by the roadside.

"How do you like the bike I got for my birthday, Uncle Angus?" I asked him.

I wasn't expecting his response.

"What are you doing down here on the Sunday? Get away home out of here."

And off back home, suitably chastened, I pedalled—hoping he wouldn't say a word to my father about it.

There was no religious bigotry, far less any religious hatred. Even in later years, as the island has become more mixed in terms of religion, we all seem to rub along fine. Arran was, is, and hopefully always will be, above all, a great place to bring up children—and for children to grow up.

My father was a remarkable man. The eldest son of a family of four girls and three boys, brought up on a rented thirty-acre smallholding, he had worked his passage to Canada by looking after Clydesdale horses on the ship carrying them across the Atlantic. He then crossed the country to Manitoba, where he worked as a shepherd, his main task being to keep the flock safe from the wolves, which were abundant—and hungry—at that time.

Canada was badly hit by the depression of the early 1930s, so on the death of his father in 1937, he returned home and took on the tenancy of Shedock Farm. He bought the farm in the early 1950s and later added the adjoining hill farm of High Balnacoole, farming three thousand acres in total, most of which was high hill sheep ground.

Like most farmers and their wives at that time, he worked every hour that God sent, resting only on a Sunday—and even that was only after the cows had been milked, fed, and mucked out in the morning, with the same chores needing done again in the evening.

I must have been a disappointment to him, as I had no interest in cattle, sheep, or anything to do with farming.

"That boy's always got his nose in a book," was not intended as a compliment, especially when there were byres to be mucked, barrows to be filled with turnips and fed to cattle, sheaves to be stooked, hay to be handled, and all the other chores familiar to anyone growing up on a family farm at that time.

My passions, when I wasn't reading, were football and—on Saturdays, as previously mentioned—going round the island on Bannatyne Motors' trucks.

The hill ground was sold a few years after my father's death, though we retained the lower ground, which became the bank's security against the borrowing necessary to fund the winkle business, with the title deeds of the farm lodged in the Bank of Scotland Head Office.

For the second half of the twentieth century, the mainspring of the Shiskine Valley was the village of Blackwaterfoot, where the Blackwater Burn, which runs through the valley, flows into the sea. This was due primarily to the efforts of four men: Lawrence and Robin Crawford, who developed the Kinloch Hotel from a small family boarding house into one of the top hotels on the island and one of two major employers in the valley; and DS and Don Bannatyne, cousins, who after finishing their National Service, formed Bannatyne Motors, for years one of the bus operators and one of the main haulage and garage services companies on the island—and the other major employer in the valley.

Vanishingly few families in Shiskine, Blackwaterfoot, and Machrie have never had at least one family member work, for a time, in one or other of those two businesses. It's sobering to think what the valley might have been like over the past seventy-five years or so, had those two businesses, with their vitality and the money they brought into the valley and paid out in wages, never existed.

Chapter 8:

Christmas 1989 had been very good for us. We had done around one hundred tons of winkles, many of them picked up by hauliers sent by the customers. It had got me thinking about the economics of the way we were doing things and whether it was still the best way forward, particularly after adverts in the West Highland Free Press brought a response from one of the two main merchants on the Isle of Skye, Carel Goodheir.

Skye is a really important source of winkles because it has such a long coastline and such a high percentage of large-sized winkles, which are the most sought after.

Before Carel came on board, we were doing about ten tons a week, but he added from two up to ten, on a really big tide. We had outgrown the small yard at Saltcoats, so when the much bigger yard next door was put up for sale, I knew I had to buy it. We needed somewhere with parking to use as our HGV Operating Centre and more space to sort out the winkles we were now receiving. Almost every morning from Monday to Saturday, there would be a line of cars parked in the street loaded with bags of winkles from local teams of pickers waiting to have them riddled (graded) and weighed in.

Inside the yard was a shed big enough to take a grader, weighers, forklifts, bags, and still leave room to store up to sixty pallets of winkles. So I paid the asking price and bought it, then immediately applied to the licensing authority to have it designated as an Operating Centre for two vehicles and to the local authority as a processing centre for the winkles. Fortunately, both applications went through with no major problems, and I was then freed from having to bring the truck back to Arran and the extra cost that entailed.

That yard would remain our operating centre for thirty years. We employed five men there on average over that period. Some were there almost from the beginning until the end, employed not to pick winkles but to buy, sort, and transport them. Most were full-time, though a few were part-time, and all were on the books, paid through the bank after tax and NI had been deducted. The reason I am emphasising that will eventually become clear.

My fortnightly round trip now was Saltcoats, Glasgow, Fife, Dundee, Tain, Glasgow, Portsmouth, Cherbourg, Hendaye, Gijon, Granada sometimes for onions, or Valencia for onions and also oranges. Then back by Barcelona, La Jonquera, Narbonne, Toulouse, Bordeaux, Cherbourg, Portsmouth, then either Birmingham, Manchester or Glasgow markets to tip, and back to Saltcoats, then home on the boat on foot.

The addition of a detour to Skye forced a decision about the transport and delivery of the winkles. It was no longer possible to do my round trip legally, that is in accordance with drivers' hours regulations, in less than a fortnight. We now had premises large enough to hold the winkles, so when Lurrietxaso, Dioni Otimende's company, said they would send a truck to pick up their winkles, I spoke to Mesguen Transport about taking the French orders on a groupage basis and gave up the trips to the continent.

Groupage refers to a lot of relatively small orders from a range of different suppliers which can all be consolidated into one load, making the transport cost economic for all concerned.

Essentially, the F7 was too lightweight for what I had been asking it to do. The inland topography of Spain is particularly hilly and hard on all aspects of a truck, and all the breakdowns I had were expensive and time-consuming. I had a clutch replaced in Cherbourg, a water pump in Perpignan, and I broke a drive shaft coupling on two separate occasions—once in Jaen, and once in Carcassonne. The brakes had failed going down a hill in Granada, and I'd had problems with the fridge in Irun, along with a myriad of smaller issues.

The return loads were barely profitable in any case, so overall I calculated we'd be better off, and I would be able to devote more time to actually managing the business, which was needed, as our sales were now over half a million pounds per year.

I would continue to collect the winkles around Scotland and the north of England for a time, but eventually Jim Cairns, who had an HGV licence, took over that job and I concentrated on managing and growing the business. In time, I asked Jim to manage the yard at Saltcoats while I ran the business mainly from Arran, though with two to three visits to Saltcoats per week. Sam Cairns, Jim's cousin, took over most of the driving. Mesguen's depot was in Glasgow, so taking the groupage orders up there became a regular event.

In conjunction with Carel Goodheir, I also eventually made arrangements with McLeods of Portree to bring the Skye winkles to Glasgow, where we could pick them up on the way back from Mesguen's depot.

After one or two bad experiences with comedians—one of whom kept me waiting in the F7 on Yorkhill Quay for a day and a half with excuses for why his truck hadn't turned up before finally admitting that actually it wouldn't be coming at all—I finally managed to find a couple of reliable haulage companies for the other Spanish orders. I also contacted a customs agent in Irun, on the France–Spain border, who would consolidate our deliveries into their own groupage deliveries along the north coast of Spain.

After buying the Saltcoats yard, we had plenty of storage for winkles. The shed could take up to sixty pallets but lacked any refrigeration. So when I saw that the administrators of a bankrupt frozen food company in the Borders were auctioning off several cold rooms, Jan and I went down the night before the sale.

Going early turned out to be a stroke of luck, because overnight it snowed and made several of the local roads difficult, so the attendance at the sale was less than it probably otherwise would have been. I bought a cold room and the associated refrigeration equipment for £1,500, about a tenth of what I thought I might have to pay.

As a bonus, we were approached by two men who said they installed cold rooms and quoted us a very attractive price to put it all together. So just in time before the warmer summer weather, we had a sixty-pallet fridge, for an overall cost of less than £5,000. One of the best investments I ever made, which would have cost around £20–30,000 if bought new, and it transformed the logistics of our buying of winkles in summer.

The added bonus for me of coming off the road was the extra time it gave me at home with Jan and the children, who were now all in their teenage years. Long-distance driving is a great job for young single men, not so good for married men with families. The time spent in the cab is time that's gone forever, and although I enjoyed my time on the road, most of the enjoyment came from the knowledge that I was building a business, in exactly the way I had planned to do it, and it was turning out to be more profitable and successful than I had ever imagined, even though my main motivation had come from being cash poor despite being asset rich on paper. You cannot live on a diet of paper.

Another benefit I had, compared with many of the guys on the road, was that I was my own boss and was always in control of my own life. One of the eye-opening things for me was the lack of respect shown to the drivers by people like receptionists of ferry companies and numerous other similar jobs, whose prevailing attitude appeared to be, whatever the facts of the situation, "Oh, the driver can wait."

Many drivers were independent-minded, self-employed men (mostly men, with very few women drivers at that time) and had taken great financial risks by leasing trucks and subcontracting work. Many were living almost hand to mouth, with the repayments on their truck to be found every month, plus the normal cost of living for themselves and their families. I thought they deserved a bit more respect from people whose idea of taking a risk in many cases would not have extended much beyond changing the colour of their hair or deciding to try to carry the bunker at the second hole rather than laying up short as usual.

Competition was fierce for the better contracts, and many seemed to spend an inordinate amount of time parked up outside bars and cafeterias, waiting for work, particularly around Valencia, where at that time, back-loads were hard to come by and many were barely profitable. Still, there was a great sense of camaraderie amongst the drivers, and you always met or passed many UK trucks on the road.

By contrast, when Jan and I drove to Almeria last year, we saw hardly any UK-plated trucks at all, and it was the same on the ferries.

When I started driving on the continent, mobile phones were very new and expensive, and not many trucks had them. In any case, they were next to useless in France and Spain, so most drivers, after leaving the ferry port, almost disappeared into a black hole as far as their bosses (and families) were concerned, uncontactable unless they chose to get in contact themselves.

Many guys, generally employed drivers, took full advantage of this situation. Indeed, it was one of the things which had attracted some in the first place, as I was told by a few. A night spent on the bevvy causing a late arrival could be, and often was, explained away to an irate boss the next day as, "Sorry guv, the policia checked my tachos and made me park up for twelve hours, nothing I could do about it." And there was nothing the boss could do about it either.

Today, it is all very different, with trucks equipped with trackers and every movement or lack of movement logged back at base.

Another characteristic of many British drivers, especially the English lads, was a determined refusal to pronounce town and city names correctly as they would be in French. So towns like Tours and Rennes, which in French are pronounced with a silent 's', would always be given a hard 's', while Nantes, pronounced 'Nont' in French, was invariably called 'Nants' with a hard 'a' and 's'. Poitiers, pronounced 'Poytee-ay' in French, was usually just called 'Potters'.

Another habit of many British drivers was to remain on UK time at all times, though that must have been pretty confusing.

As 1990 went on, we became busier and busier. Freed from the time away from the office, I was able to concentrate on sourcing new suppliers and customers.

We were now being asked to supply some of the other shellfish being exported from Scotland at that time, like lobster, velvet crab, brown crab, prawns, and cockles and mussels. There were different problems attached to each of those species which made getting involved with them problematic.

Lobster and the various crab species needed seawater facilities to be viable and probably a vivier truck (a truck with aerated tanks filled with seawater), neither of which we had—and as our Saltcoats yard was about a mile from the sea, we had no way to change that. Prawns could be dipped in a product called metabisulphate, which preserved them, but we couldn't see how we could integrate that with the winkles.

Neither cockles nor mussels were fished anywhere in the local area, and their relatively short lifespan when out of water meant they would have to be dispatched straight onto trucks more or less at the top of the beach. Experience with a couple of sample loads of cockles from teams of cockle pickers on the Solway Firth and Lancashire was not encouraging, with the required level of grading not being achieved despite assurances that it had.

From those experiences, I established what I call my rule of accountability, which states that: if there is not someone in charge, on the ground, who knows they will suffer in their pocket when shellfish are fished, loaded, paid for and dispatched remotely—i.e. unseen by the buyer—the buyer will get screwed.

This rule, suitably adapted, can be applied to many things other than shellfish, as has been seen lately in Scotland in relation to ferries.

I had become friendly with another shellfish merchant, Colin Oman, from Carradale in Argyll, though at that time living in Campbeltown, also in Argyll. We would speak almost every day on the phone and helped each other out whenever one of us was short of something or had too much of it, or just with information around prices and supply and general gossip.

Colin's main business was in velvet and brown crab and lobster, though he also bought a few winkles as well. Since most of the trade in crab and lobster around Argyll was with the Spanish trucks which arrived there every week, Colin got to hear a lot of what was happening behind the scenes, as it were. One day, he told me he had heard that a new Spanish buyer was going to be coming to Argyll and had already transferred money to a bank in Tarbert to pay for shellfish.

This buyer was Enrique Garcia, who Colin was well aware still owed me £13,000.

I asked him to try and find out which bank the money was in and immediately contacted my solicitor, who confirmed what I was hoping: that if we knew which bank the money was in, we could get a court order to freeze the money pending a court hearing to resolve the issues around the non-payment of the debt.

I bet the farm

Colin found out the bank concerned, and my solicitor got the court order freezing the money—although not without a mix-up in getting the name of the debtor, which led to an anxious twenty-four hours fretting that they would get wind and remove the money before the court order applied.

I needn't have worried. The money was frozen in Tarbert, and a date was set for a court hearing.

To cut a long story short, they didn't defend the action, and we were recompensed in full with legal costs thrown in.

A postscript to this affair came a couple of years later when I was on a sales visit to Galicia and was sitting in the waiting room of Santiago airport, prior to boarding a flight home. Who did I see through the glass into a waiting room for those waiting for flights to land but Enrique—staring at me with a look that could have frozen fire.

Chapter 9:

The Christmas market in 1990 was manic. The European winkle market at that time had several distinguishing features which may or may not have been specific to winkles but were nevertheless important to understand.

The market was structured like links in a chain. The first link was generally the first buyer from the fisherman—in this case, where all fishing was done by hand, the winkle picker. Pickers sometimes organised themselves into teams, the number in a team usually depending on how many could be carried in whatever vehicle they were using. But many pickers, particularly in more rural areas, were lone wolves, going out to the shore alone or maybe with one other person, and suiting themselves when they picked. The independence of the job was what appealed to many. I never heard of anyone actually employed to pick winkles, which is understandable when you consider the nature of the work. Winkles can only be picked at low tide, making a book of tide tables a necessary part of a picker's equipment.

Buyers like us would sometimes buy direct from the pickers, as we did at Saltcoats and one or two other places around the country. But at the scale we were now trading at, it was necessary and desirable to deal with other first buyers and what you might call team leaders—guys who, while part of a team of anything up to a dozen pickers, were acknowledged as the ones to do the bargaining with buyers like me. Then there were the travelling people, known to some as tinkers, who had a longstanding tradition of picking winkles and would often sell to the highest bidder. But I found them to be very loyal to me whenever I started to buy from them.

With the exception of some of the other first buyers, this was a cash business. You bought the winkles today; you paid cash for them today.

This led, of course, to certain problems, particularly when our customers, for the most part, either dealt directly with supermarkets—who typically didn't pay them for upwards of thirty days—or sold to customers who themselves sold to supermarkets, with the attendant delays in payment. Essentially, at the end of each week, whatever winkles we had bought in the week, we had paid for—and would not ourselves get paid for until an average of forty days later. This created a cash flow problem, which was exacerbated by the peculiar characteristics of the market from October to January.

In October, shellfish buyers who normally only bought small quantities of winkles started thinking about their supply for the Christmas market and securing that supply as far as they could. So they started pushing prices upwards. This meant that buyers like us, who bought large quantities of winkles every week, had to match those prices or risk losing supply just when we were going to need it most.

This problem was made worse by the fact that October was one of the quietest months of the year on the high streets and in the restaurants and bars of the average French and Spanish town or city, as people began to cut their spending and conserve their money for Christmas.

The point here was not just that Christmas was the most profitable time of the year for us, but it was the same for our customers—and beyond that, some of their customers, who had to have the product at that time of year and would be unforgiving of any supplier who let them down. That would inevitably have repercussions on the relationship between us and any customer who felt that we had failed them.

The solution was to use this anomaly in the relationship of price vis-à-vis supply to begin to build a stock of winkles for Christmas— something we were, for the first time, now able to do, with a capacious fridge to store them in.

We were not completely relieved of headaches with this solution, as storing the winkles was expensive. They were all paid for, yet we would not be getting paid for them until January or later, in the worst case. Also, sale and dispatch had to be carefully monitored since, although we knew that in the fridge—with plenty of cold air around them and turning over the bags every few days— they would keep well, that was only provided they had not been abused before we got them. This sometimes happened. By "abused," I mean things like them being left out in the sun or otherwise mishandled. But failing that, they would keep for up to six weeks, though careful rotation was essential when sales began to build up through November and into the manic demand of December, with the target being to obtain a clearance by the first week of January at the latest.

The bonus from finding a solution to the "October problem" was that as the buying and selling prices rose inexorably towards their peak around the 20th of December each year, we were able to benefit from selling winkles bought in October at November's prices, and those bought in November at December's prices—making December such a good month for the business.

The downside of the Christmas mania came a few weeks later, usually around the beginning of February, whenever there was a big tide and fine weather for picking. If you were not careful, you could be left with a fridge full of expensive winkles, bought at Christmas-type prices, which nobody in the whole wide world had any interest in buying—and which you would need to take a loss on, sometimes a massive loss, if you wanted to avoid having to throw them out.

It was that type of situation that prompted an Irish buyer to coin a phrase famous in the world of the winkle:

"Sure you were better looking for them than looking at them."

In any trading business where you are buying a product—any product—and reselling it, to stay solvent and hopefully be profitable, you must be able to achieve whatever margin on the buying and selling price you have calculated will cover your overheads after multiplying your margin by the volume of business you expect to do.

For me, it was essential to make, defend, and keep a margin which, when multiplied by the volume of business, was sufficient to cover all overheads. To do that, it was necessary to be able to set either the buying price or the selling price; it didn't really matter which. Otherwise, your margin could and would be squeezed. Nirvana, of course, was being able to set both prices—a state very rarely achieved, but all the more welcome when it was.

It's a really simple formula. Where A is the average selling price, B is the average buying price, C is the volume traded, and D is the overhead, then A minus B multiplied by C must be more than D, or trouble awaits. That formula, simple though it is, should work in any business buying a product then reselling it, though all products will have nuances to be taken into account. With live shellfish, that is most likely to be waste, and one of the reasons we were successful was that we managed to keep waste to an absolute minimum.

Also, I kept on top of the figures, always calculating and recalculating my average buying and selling prices, as the buying and selling prices in the market changed over time. Now that my time was mainly spent in the office managing the business, I sat down every Saturday after I had finished the paperwork for the day's dispatches and worked out our gross profit for the week on buying and selling. By five o'clock on Saturday afternoon, I knew exactly how much we had made in the week and how it related to the average overhead per week. That done, I could then enjoy the most pleasant task of the week. I would divert the office phone to my mobile and switch off the mobile until midday on Sunday.

From that point until the following Saturday evening, I was always available on the phone to suppliers, customers, and employees—any of whom were liable to ring at any time of the day or night—but that nineteen hours or so was sacrosanct and precious. Nobody other than my family was getting to me then.

Although Jan and the other girls in the office—Coral, Gina, and Marion—did all the other paperwork, I did all the pricing and invoicing for buying and selling, so I was able to keep on top of how we were doing in real time and make changes if we began to lose our way, which we would do in the near future.

The bulk of the winkles picked were consumed in France and Spain. In France, one of their principal uses was as a filler on a plateau de fruits de mer—a seafood platter. A handful or two of winkles could fill up quite a lot of space on the platter and add relatively little cost to the producer of the platter by comparison with the cost of the prawns, crab, etc., making up the bulk of it.

In Spain, while they could be used in that way, they were also consumed as tapas in bars and restaurants. There was also an important market for winkles in Holland, mainly because the Dutch were and are brilliant merchants, whatever product they are buying and selling.

Most of our customers, though not all, were producers of one or other species of shellfish, mostly oysters, mussels, or clams. Most were long established and reliable in the sense that they would pay their bills at more or less the same time every month.

I used to say to our people, and still believe, that for a trading business like ours—where everything we sell has first got to be bought and paid for—the single most important thing was not how much profit we made on a sale or how much we sold. The single most important thing was that we actually got paid.

I have had occasions where I have sold at a loss to someone who I knew would pay us, in preference to selling at a notional profit to someone who I was worried might not pay us.

In general, the most reliable customers were producers with their own extensive premises, with facilities to hold shellfish in saltwater tanks before sale. Those types of companies tended to be fairly long established, and if anything were to go wrong and they went out of business, there was something there to mitigate the damage to their creditors.

The most dangerous, as I would soon find out to my cost, often consisted of nothing more than a rented office, a telephone and fax, a list of customers, and a list of suppliers, and could be quite literally here today and gone tomorrow—leaving no forwarding address, just a trail of debt and a few angry creditors.

But sometimes, things could go wrong without any bad intent on the part of the customer.

We had a customer in France who, for weeks, was continually claiming for short weight on our deliveries. I couldn't understand it because I had met the owners, and apart from these claims—which amounted to around 150 to 200 kilos on each shipment of around four tons—I was convinced they were honest and serious businesspeople. Also, no one else amongst our customer base was having the same problem, which indicated that the issue was not at our end.

So, a week or so before Jan and I were scheduled to go to France on a selling trip, I made a point of being in Saltcoats when an order of theirs was being packed for shipment and checked that the weights were exactly right. Sure enough, a couple of days after the load was delivered, our fax fired out a claim for a credit of 160 kilos of short weight.

A couple of weeks later, we arrived at their premises about twenty minutes before noon, which is the exact time almost everybody in France—except cafés and restaurants—stop for lunch. (We were expected.) Before we sat down to lunch, I had a quiet word with one of the owners and asked him, "Who is it usually checks the weights of our deliveries of winkles?"

"Jean-Michel and Henri," he answered.

We were then introduced to all the team, so before we sat down to lunch, I said to Jan, "When I mention the weights, keep your eyes on Jean-Michel. I'll watch Henri."

So we sat down to eat and enjoyed a pleasant lunch, during which I casually enquired, of nobody in particular—though I was looking at Henri when I said it—"Who checked the weights of our last delivery of winkles?"

We both saw it—that look that can flash between two co-conspirators when a question relating to a secret they share is asked—and I knew then what the problem of the weights was. They were obviously helping themselves and probably selling what they took. A nice little earner, unknown to their employers, and what could we do about it, 600 miles away in Scotland?

After lunch, I told the owners of my suspicions, and although they were reluctant to believe me, they said they would make a point of checking for themselves on the next few shipments. We never had another claim from them, and the claim on the last shipment—the one I had personally checked at Saltcoats—was withdrawn.

Chapter 10:

1 991 began with rumours of a new inspection and regulatory regime for shellfish throughout Europe, which the authorities hoped to bring in by the end of 1992, so that all the regulatory agencies in the different EU countries were "singing from the same hymn sheet," which, on the face of it, would be a simplification and improvement on the current set-up, where each country had their own rules. As if.

As I began to realise after seeing the initial consultation documents, in many ways, this was going to create more problems for us than it solved, and I actually began to wonder if we would be able to continue operating at all, to the extent that I made enquiries about the possibility of importing winkles from Canada and, in time, visited Canada and did import a ton of Canadian winkles, though that's another story.

The main bone of contention I had with the regulations as laid out in the consultation documents was in the way they treated winkles, which are gastropods, as being similar to cockles and mussels, etc., which are bivalves. The original EEC Council Directive of 15 July 1991 (91/492 EEC) laying down the health conditions for the production and the placing on the market of live bivalve molluscs was, insofar as bivalves were concerned, a reasonable enough set of proposals. All of the EEC countries would have to regulate and approve the waters bivalves were taken from, into three grades: A, from which they could be sold direct to the public; B, from which they would have to go through a process of purification before selling to the public; and C, from which they would need to be relaid in cleaner waters before undergoing purification and only then be allowed to be sold to the public.

In addition, the premises where they could be handled before sale to the public would require to be registered with the local Health Authority (in the UK, the local council Environmental Health Department), and there were requirements for the transportation of the shellfish. It was a known fact that bivalve shellfish could be poisonous if they had come from polluted waters. (Bivalves are filter feeders, i.e., they feed by filtering the water they lie in and consuming the algae, etc., within that water.) Some kind of regulation was needed to ensure the unscrupulous minority of traders who were uncaring about whether their actions endangered public health were less likely to do so.

With all such bureaucratic proposals, the devil is usually in the detail, and so it was here. Paragraph 7 stated, "...These requirements shall apply equally to ...marine gastropods." Winkles.

As originally drafted, the regulations were actually scientifically illiterate as they included gastropods in processes, filter feeding, which they were incapable of doing.

Naturally, I was deeply concerned about the implications for our business and started to think about how I could try to ameliorate the effects it would have if introduced as planned. This involved writing to the Scottish Office of the UK government (this was pre-devolution) and eventually meeting with the Civil Servants involved along with the UK Civil Servants responsible for the UK's implementation of the regulations.

The first thing I had to do was make them aware of the winkle industry generally, never mind our place in it, as nobody in government appeared to have a clue of its existence, never mind the size of it and its importance in small coastal communities. In this I was greatly assisted by the late Dr. Eric Edwards, the Director of The Shellfish Association of Great Britain (SAGB), a man of great wisdom and experience, who, having in a previous life been a Civil Servant, was wise in the ways of government, how it worked and how those in it thought and were likely to act.

On one occasion after I had drafted a particularly fierce letter to a Civil Servant, I had the sense to run it past Eric to see what he thought, and he pointed out to me that if he had received a letter like that in his time in the Civil Service, his response would have been anything but sympathetic. He then explained how I should say the same thing without antagonising the recipient. Eric understood better than anyone the anomalous position of winkles in the Directive and was a source of great encouragement and advice in my efforts to make the powers that be aware of it too.

Eric was one of those who had conducted the experiments decades earlier which had proved that, in the words of a supportive letter he wrote to the Scottish Office Agriculture and Fisheries

Department, "The amount of heat treatment needed to extract the meat from the winkle is sufficient to sterilise the product. Furthermore, since winkles and other gastropods are not filter feeders they are exempt from the requirements of the EC designated shellfish harvesting areas." And, "In our view (the SAGB) it would be completely impractical to licence the winkle pickers. A better option is to licence the buyers of winkles who would be required to register with the local authority and meet the requirements of Schedule 3 and would be eligible to receive Permanent Transport Authorisations," which would be necessary to transport the winkles.

All this took time and money, travelling to Edinburgh and London to meet with the Civil Servants involved and was a huge distraction from running the business, even if it was ultimately successful in ensuring that the final regulations, while tiresome, were not destructive to the business I had built.

Concerning the meetings with Civil Servants, one thing that struck me was that, for many of them, whether or not their European counterparts—in particular the French—would be discomfited by anything they were to propose which in any way challenged the original Directive, seemed to be of more importance than whether or not UK businesses would be disadvantaged by not challenging the original Directive.

However, although it took about eighteen months, in the end the system as it came into being on 1 January 1993 was one we could live with, although there would be more rounds of hassle and aggravation when the EU, as the EEC became, revised the regulations in the early 2000s.

When it first aired on television, *The Apprentice* was one of my favourite programmes. I liked that the business of business was receiving some attention, but it wasn't too long before I came to dislike it intensely. The reason? Simply that many of the contestants appeared to believe that success in business was achieved by employing any means possible, not excluding stabbing in the back those who were depending on you, if that seemed advantageous, and generally behaving in an untrustworthy manner.

When we were sending away winkles we had bought and paid for with borrowed money, in the knowledge we wouldn't ourselves get paid for anything up to three months in some cases, we had to have a very high level of trust in those we were dealing with. I had come to realise that there couldn't be good business without trust, and nothing has happened since to change my mind.

Jan and I were making a lot of sales trips to France and Spain at that time in the constant search for new customers. This, of course, was in pre-internet days, when finding out about the trade overseas was a lot different from today, where a few clicks of a mouse can find you all the shellfish merchants in any given area.

We had two tactics we repeated everywhere we went in France. The first was to stay mainly in a well-known brand of budget hotels, a chain of hotels located all over France. This had two benefits. Firstly, they prepared a buffet as an option for their evening meal, which increased the odds of being able to have a good meal— not always guaranteed in budget French hotels, which generally catered for people whose tastes were different from ours.

The second benefit, and this was in the days long before mobile phones became ubiquitous, was that every one of those hotels had a telephone booth with a phone book and also a Yellow Pages for the local area. I would go in the booth and look in the Yellow Pages for the shellfish section which listed all the merchants and producers in the area and surreptitiously remove that page for further study, though sometimes I found that someone had beaten me to it and the shellfish section was already torn out.

Our other, less reprehensible method was to stop at any large supermarket we passed—Auchan, Leclerc, Super-U, Intermarché, Carrefour, you name it, we've been in it. The point of the exercise was to check the shellfish on the seafood counter, which they all have. Small shellfish are required to have a label, or *étiquette* in French, with the French name of the species, the Latin name and, crucially for us, the name and address of the producer. We would take notes of any producers of winkles we saw, whom we didn't already know, and also producers of the other species like oysters, mussels, cockles and clams, because these people often also bought winkles, even if they didn't have sales of winkles to the particular supermarket we were in.

We never at any time dealt directly with a supermarket, but many of our customers did. The extent of the control *les grandes surfaces* (the big supermarkets) exercised over their suppliers if they wanted to sell them produce was mind-boggling, mainly because of the volume they could sell, having put most of the small *poissonneries* out of business.

A customer explained it to me: "They will phone me up and say we're doing a promotion on oysters (his main business) in four weeks' time. We will need around two tons over six days, can you do that and at what price?" Two tons is a big order not to be sniffed at, so he works out that he could sell at €2.20 per kilo and have a decent profit, but he also works out that break even would be €1.50. So he calls them back and says, "OK, we could do them at €2.20."

"OK," they will say, "we'll get back to you." A few days go by and he hasn't heard back, so he calls them up and asks the buyer, "Will you want these oysters?"

"No, they're too dear, we can buy them elsewhere at under €2."

"OK," he says, "let me see what I can do and I'll get back to you." So he phones them back a couple of days later and says, "I'll do the oysters at €1.90."

To cut a long story short, after two more rounds of this they take his oysters at €1.80. But that's not the end of it. He has to deliver the oysters to the store every day. He has to supply two workers to man the stall every day for a week, and at the end of each day he has to take home any unsold oysters when he's picking up his two staff. To add insult to injury, he said, they will then take sixty days minimum to pay him.

One way or another we occasionally found good additions to our customer list, though we still landed the occasional dud.

Going to France and driving around the country visiting customers maybe sounds interesting, and I know that to many, it will sound like just another holiday, but it was quite tiring and stressful. After a few unpleasant experiences with small hire cars, I bought a succession of large, roomy, comfortable cars which made the driving more tolerable, though when we both went, Jan did most of the driving and I was the navigator.

Most of the smaller companies we visited had nobody who spoke English. My "O Level" (failed) French and Pidgin Spanish were okay for getting across what I wanted to say, but the difficult bit was understanding the replies, as once you started to speak their language, however badly, most people assumed you could understand them, which frequently wasn't the case, especially when they replied in their own language at their normal speed. The concentration necessary was extremely tiring. By the end of a day of that, and a drive of maybe two hundred miles with maybe a few wrong turns trying to find addresses you had never visited before, you definitely didn't feel like you were on holiday, though a comfortable roomy car did make a difference.

There was a postscript some years later after I had retired from the shellfish industry. I took a phone call from a chap who was selling wooden boxes which he assured me were a more sustainable alternative to the industry standard polystyrene fish boxes. Could he come to see me to discuss his boxes?

He had come to Scotland from his base in Spain and obviously had limited English. In vain I tried to explain to him that I was now retired and had no interest in his boxes, sustainable or not, and he'd be wasting his time coming to Arran, but he was insistent, said he was already on Arran and would come to the farm at two p.m., at which time he duly arrived and Jan showed him into the kitchen where I was sitting.

A man in his twenties, I thought, and he immediately went into his obviously well-rehearsed spiel, though it soon became clear that, other than a few of the basics, that was the extent of his English. As he stood there rattling off in slightly broken English all the advantages to me of his product, it occurred to me that he was probably the mirror image of how I had looked and sounded to my prospective French and Spanish customers twenty to thirty years previously.

The only difference was that, wearing a suit, he was better dressed than I had habitually been. I almost said I would take some of his boxes out of sympathy, but instead I explained as gently as I could that I was now retired from the industry and his journey had been wasted, which I could also sympathise with, having experienced the same thing many times before.

Chapter 11

In the five years or so since I had started the business, I had made plenty of mistakes, but no serious ones. Nineteen ninety-one was the year that changed, and I made my first serious, expensive mistake.

I had become friendly with a Frenchman who had a fish processing business in Troon, called Jean-Luc. Jean's business involved buying mainly prawns and fish from the boats which landed in Ayr and Troon and, after processing them, selling them to customers mainly in France but also in Spain. Jean had come to Scotland originally as a manager of a processing plant set up by the French company he worked for in France, but over time he saw the possibility of starting his own business and that's what he did.

Sometime in the middle of 1991, he asked if I could come down to his factory in Troon as he had a proposal to put to me. So I did, and found him in despair. He had no money to buy fish or to pay his rent. All his money was tied up in accounts receivable, which customers were either late in paying or had no intention of paying. Could I help him out?

He didn't need a lot of money—five thousand pounds if memory serves me—so I wrote him a cheque for that amount, for which he was grateful, and he promised he would pay it back in a month's time. A month came and went, and no sign of any money from Jean-

Luc. I didn't chase it, as I didn't need it, but a couple of months later he came to see me at Saltcoats with a greater tale of woe.

"It is for sale!"

It was all a disaster, he said. He was even deeper in the hole and didn't want to ask me to lend him any more money. Rather, he wanted me to take over the business and employ him to manage it.

I should have run a mile at the idea, but I found it attractive. We were already handling more winkles than anybody in Scotland and buying from so many different people in so many places around Britain and Northern Ireland that it was becoming difficult to find any more without effectively competing with ourselves and antagonising our existing suppliers. Further growth there looked difficult at best, and further growth was all I was interested in at that point.

There's a saying in the world of financial investment: "everyone's a genius in a bull market." A bull market is a period in the life of a stock market when the prices of stocks and shares continue inexorably upwards, and investors can easily imagine the money they're making is wholly the result of their own perspicacity, rather than as a result of their good fortune to happen to be investing during a bull market.

Since starting the business in late '85, our sales had gone inexorably upwards. But sales—particularly export sales—of all Scottish shellfish had been in a bull market, and it was my good fortune to have been in the right place at the right time to be a beneficiary.

Of course, as any striker in a football team knows, being in the right place at the right time, while being necessary to score a goal, is not sufficient. You still have to put the ball in the net, which you can't do if you're not prepared to have a go. I'd had a go with the winkles and scored, and I saw no reason why I couldn't do it again, with fish and particularly prawns, which I'd been interested in for a while—specifically, live prawns.

So, foolishly, without going over his books in forensic detail as I should have (due diligence), I agreed and so found myself once again the owner of a business I knew next to nothing about. The difference this time was that I was already all in. The amount of debt we were carrying, particularly in the months after Christmas, meant that just a few of our customers defaulting simultaneously would have left us dangerously exposed financially and put everything I owned at risk.

But this was the tail end of the Thatcher era, and though the Iron Lady was gone from Downing Street, the spirit of enterprise and risk-taking she had embodied lived on, and anything still seemed possible. So maybe I was less cautious than I should have been and put the doubts to one side.

Reality wasn't long in biting. I soon discovered that the main reason Jean-Luc wasn't getting paid by some of his customers was because some of them had claims against their invoices—usually claims concerning the quality of the product they had received—and in most cases, they had no intention of paying the invoice in full.

Complicating the situation was that, almost without exception, they either had no English or very little, which immediately vanished in a torrent of French whenever the subject of payment was broached, making Jean-Luc the only person who could have a discussion with them, which, given his part in sending them the product, was less than ideal. My French, which was usually sufficient for explaining what I thought or wanted, was unable to cope with the torrents of rapid-fire French coming down the phone whenever I asked about payment.

Jean was a lovely guy, poorly treated by some of the fishermen who took advantage of his good nature, but inclined to sometimes kid himself about stuff. He—well, we—bought trawled prawns from the local boats, which at that time were then mostly "dipped", meaning submerged in a vat of a noxious chemical called metabisulphate. This both killed and preserved them.

If they were then put into polystyrene boxes, iced over, and put in a fridge, they would keep for a few days, though ideally, they would be dispatched the same or the next day. Problems could arise if they were kept in the fridge for too long, in which case some of them would start to deteriorate and might need to be repacked, with the poorest thrown out. If this was not done, or not done thoroughly enough, when they arrived at the customer—usually at least two or three days later—there were quality problems which reduced their value.

When that happened, it was inevitable that the customer would refuse to pay the full amount of the invoice, and Jean's problem, which was now my problem, was that it happened far too often.

It took time for me to understand the full extent of the problem and the reasons for it, and during that time the financial aspect of the problem kept growing. There was another problem with Jean-Luc.

One morning he came on the phone in a panic.

"I've just had the fisheries in," he said. "They gave me a warning about buying pin hake."

Pin hake means undersized hake—a species of fish.

"Were you buying pin hake?" I asked.

"Yes, but only a few for Vispo." (Manuel Vispo, about whom more later.)

"Well, don't do it any more," I said.

"But it's really good money," he said. (Pin hake are prized in many Spanish markets, but illegal to land or to buy in Scotland.)

"I don't care how good the money is. I don't want to get involved in that."

End of conversation—but not end of story.

That was the second warning Jean had been given about buying undersized hake, and it was a final warning. It had been made clear to him—though he had neglected to tell me—that the next time, if there was one, would result in a prosecution.

This was potentially a major problem—but for me, not for Jean.

I had learned enough about Jean to know that it was entirely possible he would do it again and probably get caught again. Only this time, I would be the one in the firing line as the official owner of the offending business.

Ideally, I would have dismissed him, but I was in a trap.

We were still owed a lot of money. Despite the fact that I had managed to negotiate settlement of some of the outstanding accounts, I had very little success with the "French-speaking only" customers and felt I needed Jean-Luc if I was ever going to get their payments in.

So I decided to ask Jim Cairns to go down to Troon every day when the boats were landing—basically to keep an eye on Jean-Luc and make sure he didn't do it again.

I should have known better.

Sure enough, a few weeks later, Jean was on the phone again—very sorry, but the fisheries officers had been in again, and this time it would mean a prosecution. For me, not for him.

He had behaved himself during the day when Jim was there but had arranged for a boat to land one night with the undersized fish, which the fisheries officers had found—possibly acting on information received.

In any case, it meant I was held responsible for buying undersized fish, even though I had never seen or touched them. So I fired Jean-Luc for gross misconduct—something I should have done a few weeks earlier. I ended up paying a fine of around two hundred pounds.

As well as Jean's debts, we also, of course, had a few bad debts of our own. So we employed debt collectors to pursue the debtors and, even though we got judgements in our favour in courts in Madrid, Paris, Bilbao, and La Rochelle, the amounts of money recovered—once our costs were accounted for—was minimal.

A typical example was one of Jean-Luc's customers in Rungis in Paris. When the officers appointed by the court went to their office, after obtaining entry, they found a small office empty but for a couple of desks, a few chairs, a disconnected telephone, a Paris phone book, and a few empty cigarette packets.

In total, bad debt from the Jean-Luc episode alone came to around one hundred thousand pounds, which we wrote off over five years.

In any event, as Christmas 1991 was fast approaching, our trade in winkles was explosive again, and I really didn't have the time or the energy to sort Troon out any more than I already had by parting company with Jean and putting Richmond Murphy—a former fisherman from Kintyre, who was very reliable—in charge.

In November, we sold one hundred and three tons of winkles, the first time we had ever done one hundred tons in any month other than December.

On Saturday, 7 December, we sent away forty-nine tons—the most we'd ever done in one day—and we ended the month having sold one hundred and fifty-six tons, our best month ever in terms of both sales and profitability.

Though extremely worrying, as we had paid for every bag by the end of the month, we would have to wait till February at least to be sure we would get paid for what we'd sold. I was now extremely conscious of the danger of bad debt.

There were a couple of other reasons why I had been attracted to Jean's offer to take over his business. I had been thinking about getting involved in prawns for a while, but specifically live prawns, for which I had several potential customers. Also, just along the harbour at Troon were shellfish purification tanks, which had lain empty and unused for a number of years, and which I knew could be used for "crawling" winkles. These were owned by ABP, the owners of Jean-Luc's yard, which I was now renting from them.

I had been contacted by a guy from around Fort William, David Clark, who had assured me he could buy live prawns on a regular basis. All creeled, caught by fishermen in pots called creels which they lower to the seabed for the prawns to go into. Creeled prawns are stronger than trawled prawns, which most of those landed at

Troon were at that time, and better able to survive for the time necessary to reach their final destination, usually Spain.

I had also been contacted by a woman from Galicia, in Northern Spain, Angela Gonzalez, who was keen to buy live prawns and wanted them air-freighted to Santiago de Compostela, as many as we could send.

So I financed Clark to buy the prawns and hired him a fridge van to transport them in. We set up a water cascade system in the Troon factory to refresh them after he delivered them, since by then they had been out of the water about five hours.

The first problem with this set-up was one of logistics, as we needed to handle, pack, and transport the prawns to Glasgow Airport by three a.m. for onward shipment to Heathrow, from where they would be flown to Santiago. The main problem was that the team needed for this operation were essentially the same people who had been dipping and packing the trawled prawns the previous morning. Most of them were women who hadn't the time nor desire to do a shift from ten a.m. till around three p.m., then come back for another one from ten p.m. till past midnight.

We had tried to find more packers, but without much success. A particular problem was the unwillingness of many potential employees to go "on the books" for fear of losing their benefits, and my reluctance to employ people off the books. Some insisted they got no benefits and were self-employed, though that necessitated a form which they never seemed able to supply, something that would come back to haunt me years later, despite us firing them if they couldn't provide the correct paperwork after four weeks.

Having spent a couple of weeks in Troon staying in the Anchorage Hotel, I could appreciate the problem. After taking the prawns to the airport myself and arriving back at around four in the morning, then rising around eight to go up to Saltcoats for a day's work there, a few times, I could see that it was unsustainable in the long run.

Soon another problem reared its head, one which, though I couldn't yet know it, would cause me headaches years into the future: Heathrow. The prawns which in the winter months had been arriving in Santiago full of life and in top condition, were now arriving with some either dead or dying.

I checked all through the transport process, and it soon became clear that the problem was at Heathrow, where the boxes would sometimes sit for hours on the tarmac no matter the weather conditions. The facilities there, I am told, are greatly improved now with capacious refrigerated hangars for our kind of products, but at that time, once the weather heated up, what happened to your goods was a lottery.

We were turning over a lot of money at Troon, but that was about all we were doing. What with Jean-Luc's existing bad debt and one or two more that we incurred ourselves, plus the labour problems and the capriciousness of some of the suppliers, who always seemed to have prawns when they weren't needed, yet never seemed to have them when they were, as the summer of 1992 wore on, I began to think we were wasting our time in the prawn business.

The Jean-Luc, Troon, bad debt experience had clarified my thinking about how I wanted the business to progress in the coming few years.

At first, before I fully understood the extent of the problems at Troon, I had thought that we could perhaps make a quantum leap in the amount of business we were doing, with prawns and possibly crab and lobster etc added to our existing trade in the winkles. I had realised that though it could be done, it couldn't be done from Arran, and if I did want to expand in that way, I would need to leave Arran and live most, if not all, of my life somewhere on the mainland, something I had no desire to do, so that I could be on top of all aspects of the business on a daily basis. I was from Arran, my family and friends were on Arran, and that was where my life outside the shellfish business was, including the farming business with my brother Charlie.

The amounts of money which would be involved, with its attendant risks, precluded trying to make it work from Arran; it would almost certainly have failed and been financially disastrous, in other words, an inadvisable gamble with a ratio of risk to reward which was the opposite of what I knew to be the key metric for the success of my business. Alternatively, I could have appointed a manager to run the Troon operation, if I could have found one with all the necessary skills to do so, but lacking the ambition to see my business as a stepping stone toward establishing his own business, possibly with my suppliers and customers. Even if I had found such a person, by the time I had paid him, we would have needed to substantially increase the volume of business with all the increased risk that would have brought in a branch of the industry whose customers, by their nature, tended to be fairly risky enterprises, as the Jean-Luc experience had already shown. So neither was that a realistic option in my opinion.

So far I had, as it were, bet the farm, going into debt, confident the odds were in my favour with the winkle business and come out ahead with a good solid business which I was confident would continue to prosper without me needing to take any unnecessary risks. So, with renewed certainty, I resolved to concentrate mainly on the winkles, in which we now had a dominant position in the market, which I was confident I could do from Arran with visits to Saltcoats and Troon a few times each week.

That was how we ran the business successfully for the next fifteen years, until we got involved with razor clams: but that's another story.

So, somewhat reluctantly, I decided to close the Troon factory we had taken over from Jean-Luc and leave prawns alone for now, but agreed a rental with ABP for the aforementioned premises with the seawater tanks, as it was becoming clearer how the new regulations due at the end of the year would work and that with a bit of investment in pumps etc. we would be able to crawl winkles in the tanks and sell directly into markets which up till now had been closed to us, provided we could get the premises approved, which we did at the beginning of 1993, just as the new regulations came into force.

I was disappointed with the way the prawn venture had turned out but there was a limit to the risks I was prepared to take and in Troon I had discovered my limit and the point at which for the first time since starting the shellfish business, I had favoured discretion over valour. Or, as some might have put it, for the first time favoured sense over stupidity.

In any case, during that financial year of 1991–92, we had our best ever sales of £1,616,468, which, according to the official Bank of England inflation calculator, would be worth over £3.5 million at the time of writing, April 2025.

Chapter 12:

In 1992 we had started to buy winkles from an Irishman, Henry Donnelly, from Carlingford in County Louth. Henry was working for a relative, Paul Clark, who was wanting to retire and sell his shellfish business. As time went on we were getting more and more from Henry, who was going above and beyond in searching out winkles of good quality, but paperwork around the transport was a problem and there were other possibilities in other species in that part of Ireland.

So Jan and I travelled to Carlingford, and after some discussion and negotiation, we bought Paul Clark's business and formed a limited company, Carlingford Shellfish Ltd, which would supply Sandy MacAlister Shellfish with winkles. It solved the paperwork problem, and we worked together successfully for over twenty years, remaining friends still.

Another reason to follow this path was as a possible alternative way to continue in business should the UK authorities fail to introduce the new regulations in a sensible manner. I felt, from speaking to our main Irish competitors, that the Irish authorities had a more relaxed and sympathetic approach to the whole subject of shellfish and indeed business regulation.

I needn't have worried about our Health Authorities; they eventually brought in the new regs sensitively and sensibly. I didn't yet know it, but in time, I would discover the agency I really should have been worried about was the Inland Revenue.

The months before Christmas 1992 were, for me, dominated by my efforts to get some sense into the new regulations as they would apply to winkles in the UK. Following is from a letter I wrote to the Scottish Office Department of Agriculture and Fisheries regarding these regulations.

"Dear Sir,

Following my several phone calls concerning EC Regulation 492, the following is a summary of the situation as it appears to me with regard to winkles.

Firstly, some background to the current position. The winkle industry in Scotland represents all or—in most cases—part of the income of approximately 2,000 people around the country. Picking winkles is usually seen as a means of supplementing another income or as a component part of an income derived from various sources, as in the case of crofters, etc.

In consequence, the industry contributes to and sustains the fabric of life in a great many of the most isolated and disadvantaged communities around the country, particularly in the Highlands and Islands."

The crux of the problem was that the regulations as proposed by Brussels were, in their treatment of winkles, fundamentally scientifically illiterate. Within them was a requirement for winkles to undergo purification similar to that for bivalves before they could be sold to the public, unless they had been picked in clean (Grade A) waters.

But winkles, not being filter feeders, cannot be purified in that way. That meant that only winkles from A-grade waters could legally be placed on the market.

But the classification of waters into A, B, and C grades, supposed to be carried out by Local Authorities in the UK, on which the entire system was based, could not apply to every nook and cranny of the Scottish coastline by virtue of the cost to the LAs. But since it was in those nooks and crannies that most Scottish winkles were picked, a Kafkaesque situation was being created where, to follow the regulations to the letter of one part of the law—i.e., declare exactly where you had picked your winkles—meant you wouldn't be able to get a health certificate (renamed a movement document), making them unsaleable.

The most likely outcome was that a black market would be created, and the intention of the policy—to regulate the trade—would be subverted, thus rendering the entire expensive, bureaucratic exercise pointless while criminalising almost everyone involved in the trade.

Another problem, as I discovered when representing the interests of the winkle industry at a meeting in London with the Ministry of Agriculture Fisheries and Food, was UK officialdom's lack of knowledge of our industry's existence, never mind its size.

The MAFF people thought that the main interest in the new regulatory regime, from a Scottish point of view, would be in respect of the relatively new Scottish mussel industry. They were flabbergasted when I pointed out that Sandy MacAlister Shellfish alone had exported more tons of winkles in the past year than the entire Scottish mussel industry had exported of their product, and that furthermore, others were also involved in exporting winkles, so our industry's total exports were, at that time, financially, much more valuable to UK Plc.

Eventually, mainly thanks to the efforts of Eric Edwards and the SAGB, sense prevailed, and a workable system was enacted, partly dependent on Tippex, faxes, and officialdom judiciously turning a blind eye when necessary, allowing the trade to continue much as before.

During the time in between the full potential horror of the EC regulations becoming clear and good sense prevailing, I felt I had to make a contingency plan for how we could continue the business if our supply of winkles was to dry up, notwithstanding the Irish company might be caught in the same stramash.

So I made enquiries and studied the distribution of winkles around the world, finally deciding the only realistic alternative source of supply was North America, specifically Canada.

I researched the Canadian winkle business and concluded the best possibilities were in the Province of New Brunswick. I got in touch with a couple of merchants there and booked flights for Jan and I to visit them, flying in September 1992 from Glasgow to Toronto then from Toronto to St John, capital of New Brunswick.

What we did discover was that the Canadian winkles were of very good size and quality and could be commercially viable if we had to pivot in that direction, though the available quantities would be nothing like we were used to. The price would also be viable, though we would have been looking at a much smaller business overall. In the event, we did buy and import a one-ton pallet, though that created another unforeseen problem.

When we notified our Environmental Health Officer (EHO) about the imported winkles, they—as was their duty—informed the Scottish Office in Edinburgh. That stirred up a hornets' nest of concern about something we had known nothing about previously. Some people in the Scottish Office got really het up about the Canadian winkles and, as soon as they heard about them, rushed over to Saltcoats to inspect them and tell us that on no account should they be relaid in Scottish waters, something we never had any intention of doing anyway. They were concerned that some Canadian disease of the winkles might contaminate the pristine Scottish waters, though they appeared not to have any specific disease in mind.

Because we had never intended to relay them anyway, I hadn't given any thought to this. I had thought our only problem might be with our EHO, but Environmental Health had no concerns because we had a Canadian Health Certificate for the shipment.

One of the most important people in the success or otherwise of a business like ours, handling what were foodstuffs, was our local EHO, who had the authority to close us down if they saw fit. I still consider us to have been extremely fortunate to have had, for the most part, good sensible EHOs who saw their job as assisting businesses such as ours to comply with the laws and regulations, enabling us to continue to feed wages, etc., into the local economy— to the people who ultimately employed them—rather than enforcing the letter of the law irrespective of the economic consequences or common sense.

I was probably helped in rubbing along with the various EHOs by always bearing in mind, in my dealings with them, a piece of wisdom I was given by Willie Kerr, plumber and builder late of this parish, who once told me in reference to the Local Council Clerk of Works—I think that was this guy's title—"these folk," said Willie, "can be a right pain in the neck, but you have to give them their place." Conscious of the reality that "these folk" could close my business down, I always made sure I gave them their place, and I never really had much bother, with one exception.

From time to time, I heard stories of other EHOs in other parts of the UK whose attitude seemed to be almost to make the lives of those running businesses as difficult as possible, quite often because their understanding of the regulations they were charged with enforcing was incomplete or even just plain wrong.

Once the new regulations were finally passed, I made it my business to obtain a copy and read every word pertaining to winkles to the point where I could quote chapter and verse, off the top of my head, if I needed to. On more than one occasion, I was able to advise other merchants that what they were being told by their EHO was not in the legislation and consequently they had no need to do what they were being told to do.

That wasn't purely altruistic since problems seemed to come mostly from one EHO getting an idea in their head, then asking others at the regular meetings they had why they were not doing the same thing, then some of them going home and telling merchants they should be doing this or that. So anything which lessened the chances of unnecessary problems occurring was worthwhile.

One such hullabaloo erupted over labelling and transport. All premises where live shellfish were handled, such as our yard at Saltcoats, were designated as Dispatch Centres and given a number. Every country all across Europe did the same. The regulations mandated that each Dispatch Centre could only accept shellfish from either grade A waters or a registered Purification Centre, and each batch of shellfish had to be accompanied by a Registration Document.

This made no allowance for the fact that much of the Intra-Europe trade in shellfish was from merchant to merchant—for example, a merchant in Scotland selling to a merchant in France, both of them now operating Dispatch Centres. But on the

Registration Document would be the name and address of the fisherman (the Gatherer in EC reg speak), their contact details, and where they had fished the shellfish.

This was anathema to the originating merchant because he knew that once his customers had these details, there was a decent chance they would contact the fishermen themselves and cut him out, a potential outcome which had clearly not occurred to those drawing up the legislation.

The solution involved imaginative and varying interpretations of such words and expressions as "batches," "placing on the market," and "conditioning," which, while not strictly in keeping with the legislation as originally laid down, enabled the trade to continue without too much disruption. An all-too-rare success for pragmatism over bureaucracy.

Incidentally, for anyone wondering why it always appeared to be just me arguing the case with officialdom concerning the rules and regulations around winkles and thinking there must have been others or some producers organisation, or similar, also involved; well there wasn't. The only organisation with any interest in the winkles, their pickers, or their buyers and sellers, was the Shellfish Association of Great Britain (SAGB), at that time headed by the aforementioned Dr Eric Edwards.

Eric was immensely helpful and unofficially co-opted me to speak to officialdom on the subject of the winkles on behalf of the SAGB. Winkles were of little interest to the majority of his members, who were based in England and primarily interested in bivalves and crustaceans. If any other Scottish merchants were making a case for the winkle industry, I never heard anything about it or them.

I had to involve myself in those discussions, since, as the biggest trader in winkles, I had most to lose if unsuitable regulations were adopted. In addition, at that time our business was mainly dependent on winkles, whereas most other Scottish merchants traded mainly in crustaceans like crab and lobster or bivalves like mussels, with winkles forming only a relatively small part of their overall business.

Our main competitors now, in the French market, were the Irish, particularly the two biggest Irish exporters of winkles: Mulloy Shellfish, run by Andy Mulloy, and Carrowholly Shellfish, run by George Golden, both companies located in Westport, County Mayo. I spoke with both of them from time to time, as the things which were affecting us would usually impact them too, particularly the European regulations.

Prices were always of interest, particularly selling prices, though they had always had an advantage over us in that the Irish Pound (commonly known as the Punt) generally traded at around a 10% discount to the British Pound.

In practice, what tended to happen, in the winkle market at any rate, was that when winkles were plentiful and difficult to sell, the Irish could sell at around 10% cheaper than us in French Francs, thus making their product more attractive to the French. But when winkles were scarce, they could sell at the same price as us in Francs, thus increasing their profit. Fortunately we saw little of them in the Spanish market at that time.

Christmas 1992 was another record breaker, though it started off slowly as we tried to build a stock in October. The weather in early October was poor, reducing the availability of winkles, so we ended the month with very little stock. However, a good tide at the end of October with some welcome good weather meant we went into November with about 40 tons in stock, and we built that up through the month with winkles stacked high on the pallets in the fridge and the boys complaining about the work involved in periodically rebuilding them so the bags could be turned.

We sold 102 tons in November, and I could see that money was going to be tight by the end of December. We had customers old and new, and others we had hardly ever heard of, phoning and faxing desperate for winkles for Christmas, since word had obviously got around that we were the place to go for them. Sas de Koier of Kopek BV told me he had been told that "Sandy MacAlister has bought every winkle in Scotland." Not quite accurate, though we definitely had bought more than what many would consider our fair share.

I had thought we might get over 200 tons for the month, but in the end, we only managed 177 tons for December. It was probably just as well. The combination of paying for the winkles when we bought them but not getting paid for, on average, 45 days meant we were £250,000 overdrawn and faced an anxious wait until about mid-February before we could be fairly sure that the month had indeed been profitable.

As it turned out, we mostly got paid that year, but little did we know that the following year would be very different.

Chapter 13:

My main concern as the new year began was financial, with several court cases ongoing in various courts all over France and Spain, most of them hangovers from the Jean-Luc experience.

We had given the bad debt accounts to a firm of debt collectors, who had proven to be worse than useless. They had assured us they could find solutions, in the knowledge that all the accounts were with companies in France and Spain. When after two months we chased them with questions about progress, we were staggered to learn that they had made no progress at all. The reason? Every time they had written, they had no reply. Unbelievably, all their letters were in English—to people who they had been told either spoke no English or affected to speak no English!

To add insult to injury, they wanted a percentage of what we had managed to extract from one company entirely by our own efforts, which had involved paying a company to translate all the communications to and from the debtor.

They were all now in the hands of Dun & Bradstreet, experienced debt collectors who were pursuing our money in court in La Rochelle, Bilbao, Rennes, Madrid, and also Manuel Vispo's company, which we used a Spanish lawyer to pursue, for reasons which I can't quite remember now, though possibly because for some reason they couldn't actually be taken to court.

Some of those accounts went back to the early days of 1991, so were extremely frustrating, particularly since some of them were undefended and we had judgements in our favour. We never actually saw very much money from those cases even though we won almost all of them—they were mostly pyrrhic victories, providing only the satisfaction of knowing that we had done all we could, as the money recovered was minor after deducting costs.

The new shellfish regime had begun on 1 January 1993 in tandem with the European Single Market, designed to make it as easy to sell and send goods from Saltcoats to Santander as to Southampton. For us, the main change that January should have been that we now had the premises at Troon operational, where we could crawl winkles, which had a couple of advantages. We could now sell to customers such as those in markets like Paris Rungis and MercaMadrid, which opened up new possibilities. And secondly, we could revive winkles which otherwise might have been lost and had to be thrown out, particularly in summer.

But a new problem had reared its head. We had been visited at Saltcoats by two of the Cunninghame District Council (CDC) EHOs, who informed us that we had to keep a register of pickers, where they picked, and how much they had picked—a level of record-keeping which I couldn't see mandated in the new regulations. This would create an extra layer of unwanted and unnecessary bureaucracy which I was sure wasn't in the regulations.

So I spoke to two other merchants in Scotland and our main competitors in Ireland and established that none of them had been given the same requirement by their Health Departments. Then, I phoned our local EH office and said it was unacceptable, as it wasn't required by the regulations, and would not apply to any of our competitors, which would put us at a competitive disadvantage.

The following day, I phoned again to see if there was any progress and was told they were writing to Edinburgh for confirmation of the situation regarding record-keeping. Later that day, one of the EHOs phoned to say that, according to his reading of the regulations, we were required to follow their instructions. As he spoke, I realised he was not reading from the same regulations as I had seen, and after a few questions, he admitted he had not actually seen, never mind read, the final operative legislation but was working from an earlier draft version.

Once again, I enlisted the assistance of Eric Edwards at the SAGB and, on his advice, phoned my contact in the Scottish Office in Edinburgh, who promised to look into the matter. This was all a problem, as it was holding up the issue of our official EC registration number from CDC, without which we could no longer operate legally, so it had to be fixed ASAP.

I then discovered that CDC had informed Edinburgh that we were not prepared to test winkles (incorrect) as well as not prepared to keep a register (correct). I wrote to Edinburgh to correct the factual errors and any false impression created.

When I again pressed for the Registration Number to be issued, CDC's head office in Irvine then claimed to have legal advice backing their EHO's interpretation of the legislation. But I learned from our local office that the problem was that Irvine simply didn't want to admit they were wrong and were scratching around trying to find a way of saving face.

Eventually, the Registration Number was issued, without any requirement to keep the records originally requested nor any apology for the error or the time, trouble, and expense I had to go to, to school them on their own legislation.

It was the only time I had ever been told by an EHO, "We will enforce the legislation and if you don't comply, you won't be able to operate," despite the fact that he was never able to show me where in the relevant legislation it said I had to do as he said. "Because I say so" has never worked too well with me.

Troon was under Kyle and Carrick District Council (KCDC) and, in the early part of the year, was approved under a temporary derogation from the regulations which allowed us to operate in the meantime. They were always courteous and helpful, and we obtained our final approval in December.

1994

Late in 1993, it was suggested to me that we should enter that year's competition for the UK Department of Trade and Industry (DTI) Export Awards for small businesses of under 200 employees. I did this without much expectation of success, as it was UK-wide and apparently normally attracted over 200 entrants. Anyhow, I filled out an application form and sent it off.

The year rolled on uneventfully until December, when we finally cracked the 200 tons per month barrier, selling 212 tons for the month.

Early in 1994, we were notified that we had made the shortlist for the DTI awards and were asked to supply an auditor's certificate verifying our financial figures, management accounts, and a geographical breakdown of our exports for the past two years. We sent it all off at the end of April and were delighted to hear at the end of June that we had been awarded a Certificate of Merit, to be announced and presented later in the year, recognising our achievement in increasing our export sales by so much.

As the year progressed, I was becoming more and more concerned about our overall profitability. We had increased our sales to the point where we now had approximately 25% of the entire European market for winkles and were almost certainly selling more winkles than anyone else in the world—the European market being larger than all the rest added together, as I had discovered when researching Canada and other possible alternative sources of supply.

So, realistically, we couldn't increase sales by much more without finding we were competing with our existing customers. Yet, particularly after taking into account the bad debts, our overall profitability was declining rather than increasing.

So I looked at cutting costs, and we trimmed a few things, but it was increasingly apparent that our overheads, which had crept up and up over the past few years, would need to have an axe taken to them to make an appreciable difference. The overheads we had taken on when taking over Jean Luc's operation at Troon had never really been adjusted to take account of the reduction in workload there, after we shut it down.

The new premises there for crawling the winkles really could be run as a one-man operation with occasional help, so to put it bluntly, the only way to cut overheads in any meaningful way was through redundancies, but I was reluctant to do that—probably for too long.

Now that we had the tanks at Troon up and running with full EH approval and could look seriously for a customer list for the crawled winkles, Jan and I needed to step up our search, so we travelled to France and Spain a couple of times that spring. The biggest problem, since we were looking for clients at a different level from most of our existing customers (by which I mean they tended to be customers of our existing customers or their competitors), meant there were political issues which had not been so important previously and we had to proceed with extreme care.

Ultimately, there was no point in securing a new client who bought 300 kilos a week, albeit at a better profit, if it took that customer away from an existing customer who bought three tons a week and would almost certainly be disgruntled, probably to the point of finding a new supplier.

So, many mornings were spent rising around 5 am to visit fish markets and check out the sellers of winkles—firstly to establish who their supplier was, and then, if that supplier wasn't one of our existing customers, to try to interest them in our winkles.

Taken from Arran Banner article on Export Award
Photograph: Arran Banner

A tip for anyone visiting a fish market: never go without your wellies or you will stink of fish all day. All fish markets use a lot of ice, particularly in the boxes of fish, which melts and is almost impossible to avoid getting on your footwear. The smell of fish will also cling to your clothes, but you can wash them and it's gone. It's more difficult to remove it from your shoes.

We spent a lot of time also visiting supermarkets, checking the labels on the displays of winkles and visiting their suppliers, if appropriate. It wasn't all work of course, and it was interesting and educational visiting new places and comparing towns, cities, infrastructure, etc. with home.

We found a good customer in Santander, which along with San Sebastian and the Rias Baixas area of Galicia—particularly the Isla de Arousa, near to Cambados, one of the centres of the Spanish mussel industry—were probably our favourite Spanish areas.

Galicia, particularly out of tourist season when it's not snarled up with traffic, is beautiful, reminiscent of home, just without the rain with which we are so familiar, though they think they have a wet climate, which they do, relative to other parts of Spain, though nothing like the West of Scotland.

Asturias, which we often passed through on our way to and from Galicia, always reminded me of how I imagined Middle Earth from Tolkien's *Lord of the Rings*, with its small fields usually bordered by hedges and the red-tiled roofs of the farmhouses with their traditional *horreos* (granaries).

Most of our time in France was spent in Brittany, the epicentre of the French shellfish industry, and Normandy, which we visited regularly as we usually travelled by the Portsmouth–Cherbourg ferry. Our favourite small French city was probably Quimper, a beautiful small city near the south-western tip of Brittany and close to a very good customer in La Forêt-Fouesnant on the coast.

One of the characteristics of the shellfish business, which may for all I know be common to all trading businesses, is that if you are a reliable supplier of a product, as we were with winkles, you will occasionally be asked to supply similar products which you don't trade in.

It works like this. A customer phones you up one day and asks, "Can you get me some of a product?" It might be mussels or cockles or clams or whatever. You say, "What price would you pay?" He tells you, and then you say, "OK, I'll see what I can do." You then start phoning around everybody you know who sometimes has the product requested.

The usual response is, "Well, they're a bit scarce just now. How much would you pay?" You quote the price you've been given— obviously with a bit deducted for your profit—and then they usually say, "Well, I'll see what I can do, but I doubt that price will cut it." So you say, "OK, do what you can," hang up, and repeat the exercise with as many potential suppliers as you know.

All this takes time and effort and yields nothing until one day, one or more of the people you've called phones up and says, "These cockles, mussels, clams, whatever, you were looking for a couple of weeks ago—I could do you some now." "Oh," you say, "at the price we spoke about?" "Aye, no problem. When do you want them?" So you hang up, phone the customer who'd made the original request and tell him you've got these cockles, mussels, clams, whatever he was looking for at the price he quoted you, only to be told, "No chance. The market's glutted now. Everybody's got them. Sorry, we don't need them now."

So then you have to go back to the supplier and tell him, "Sorry, I don't need them now. Everybody's got them, apparently." Everybody—but especially you—has wasted a great deal of time, possibly damaged a few relationships along the way, and profited by precisely nothing.

So what has occurred? Cockles, mussels, clams—whatever—were for one reason or another scarce. Nobody had them, so the merchants whose customers expect them to always have them have called everybody they know who might be able to get them and asked them to "see what they could do." All those people have gone looking, discovered the product isn't available for whatever reason, but placed provisional orders for when it is available. Eventually, the product has come back on stream, all the merchants who usually trade in it have got what they need from their usual suppliers, and they no longer need anything from those they contacted in desperation. Those people now have to deal with the consequences of asking other people to find the product for them, now that they are calling trying to move the product—which everyone now has and nobody really wants any longer.

Ready to roll again

Checking the load at South Queensferry

Eventually, you learn to recognise the situation and just ignore any such requests. I used to sum it up by saying, "It's difficult to make money from something you're not at," which seems beyond obvious but was meant to reflect the type of situation I've just described.

Another recurrent problem, and one impossible to ignore, was the occasional glut of winkles in the market. Typically, a glut would arrive a couple of weeks or so after a big tide which had coincided with high pressure and good weather. If you were not very careful, you could end up with a fridge full of winkles that nobody in the world wanted.

Particularly dangerous were gluts which either arrived when the weather was hot and sunny, or arrived when winkles were very expensive—since the glut was certain to cause prices to plummet, meaning losses were guaranteed.

The former situation was less common and also less predictable. You could predict the tides accurately, and the first thing I did every year was transcribe the tide tables, which are accurate predictions of the times and height of high and low tides at different locations around the UK coast, into my diary, which was my constant companion throughout the year.

So the trick was to pay close attention to the weather forecast and, using that in combination with the tide tables, try to predict the future supply around the country and prepare accordingly, something I had needed to become quite good at.

Preparation for a glut, I found to be one of the most stressful situations over the years, but it had to be done, or else you could be left with horrendous losses. It involved speaking to all our suppliers and either chopping the price we were paying them, which meant they would have to do the same with their suppliers, or putting them on a quota—i.e., where we might usually take five tons from them, we would limit them to one or two tons, the amount depending on the likely quality of their winkles—or, in extremis, I might have to tell them we couldn't take anything at all this tide.

Naturally, these were difficult conversations, as I was effectively telling them their income over the next few weeks was going to be much reduced and that they, in their turn, were going to need to have the same stressful conversations with the guys they were buying from.

Of course, theoretically, they still had the option of selling elsewhere, but they all knew that if I wasn't buying, every other buyer would almost certainly be in the same position. A glut sometime in the period from February to April was almost guaranteed every year. The difficulty was in predicting exactly when.

With prices being so high over Christmas and New Year, when January came, despite the usually colder weather, most winkle pickers wanted to be out picking for as long as the high prices continued. The problem for me was that prices in the main European markets reduced, sometimes very quickly, after New Year, and you could, if you weren't careful, end up losing money on everything you were buying.

But at least that kind of seasonal glut was to a certain extent predictable, and even if you got stuck with a lot of expensive winkles, they were generally in good condition and could be sold eventually, even if at a loss.

Much more dangerous and generally costly, though rare for obvious reasons—we live in Scotland—was the glut which arrived out of the blue after a spell of hot summer weather around the time of a very big tide. The problem here was twofold. Firstly, it was difficult to predict and therefore to take the appropriate precautions for. Secondly, the winkles were much more likely to be in poor condition, having often been exposed to the heat by the pickers themselves, many of whom kept them in less than ideal conditions, sometimes for more than a week before selling them, so that by the time we received them, irreversible deterioration had set in. Though they were still alive when we got them, they were unsaleable, as our customers would almost certainly reject them.

Unless there were dead winkles in the bags when we received them from our regular suppliers, it was my policy to take any losses on the chin rather than refuse to pay for them, even though it was tough to take. My reasoning was that if I penalised a supplier for something which was fundamentally beyond his control now—even though I could have done that—it was less likely he would still be there when I needed his winkles in wintertime. Discretion being the better part of valour, you could say, which was probably the reason he had bought them originally.

Where I drew the line was this: if I could put my hand into a bag, take out a handful of winkles, and find one dead winkle, it was as near certain as made no difference that there were a lot more dead winkles in the bag. Given that a 25-kilo bag could contain over 5,000 individual winkles, and if I could do that, the supplier should have been able to do the same and therefore should have known not to buy the winkles in the first place.

My philosophy was that while it would have been easy to maximise profit by squeezing my suppliers in summertime when winkles were harder to sell, and to squeeze my customers in winter, particularly around Christmas time when winkles were in high demand, it was better to look after my regular suppliers in summer. I never left them with unsold winkles no matter how difficult they were to sell, unless they had ignored my warning that a glut was coming and had massively gone over the quota I'd given them. In turn, I would prioritise and look after my regular customers around Christmas when I knew they really needed to have winkles, by not slipping away and selling to the non-regulars who always came looking at that time, offering well above the going price just to get their hands on some winkles.

Occasionally, someone I knew would come back from a holiday in France or Spain—sometimes a winkle picker—telling me about the price they had seen winkles on sale at in a market or supermarket or fishmonger's. I really didn't care how much profit was made on them after we had sold them. I always knew what we needed to make on them and what was achievable, and as long as I was happy with the price I got, what the next man got was his business. If he made money, he was more likely to come back for more.

Up to the point of taking over Jean-Luc's business, I had never considered insuring our sales against the customers defaulting, but that experience caused me to look hard at the possibility of doing so in future. I could see the benefits of it and the possible cost-effectiveness of it, but in the end, I rejected the idea. My main problem with insurance was that the insurers wanted all of our customers insured, not just the ones we wanted to insure.

At that time, I had full confidence in all of our biggest and most important customers and didn't fancy paying a percentage of our sales to insurers. I have never regretted that decision. What we would have paid out in insurance over the next twenty years or so would have dwarfed what we lost thereafter in bad debt, by the simple expedient of paying really careful attention to the type of people we were dealing with and not doing business with any who didn't pass the two tests I had for trustworthiness.

Those went like this. I liked to sit across a table from anyone I was considering selling to and look them in the eyes when terms of business etc. were being discussed. I had learned to recognise the bullshitter's look—the brazen stare into your eyes which is looking to see whether their nonsense is being believed and calculating how far they can go and how much they can pile it on.

The second test was the price acceptance test. I came to understand that if you quote someone a price above the prevailing market price and they accept it and agree to pay it without questioning or challenging it, then very possibly it is because they have no intention of paying it at all or, at best, intend finding some spurious reason for demanding a credit on your invoice. That type of customer I wanted nothing to do with after the Jean-Luc experience.

As 1994 wore on, we had more and more issues with our premises, both at Saltcoats and at Troon. Although we had our approvals in place for both locations, those approvals were dependent on us carrying out a programme of upgrading to bring them up to the standards mandated in the EC regulations.

Some of the work we could do ourselves, but other elements required outside contractors, adding significant expense. Some requirements seemed especially pointless, such as moving the compressors for the fridge room from the ground up onto the roof of the fridge—a costly manoeuvre involving rewiring and structural modifications.

When you hire a joiner to hang a door, or a plumber to fix a leak under your sink, you generally know what needs to be done, how long it should take, and whether the tradesman is taking you for a ride. How many people, though, know anything about industrial refrigeration?

How many can say with confidence, as they watch a refrigeration engineer wandering around a fridge room humming and hawing to himself for hours on end, whether or not that person is being genuine? Not many of us. I don't like to think about how much money was wasted in those early years, until I finally asked the refrigeration engineers on Arran to take over responsibility for the Saltcoats fridge.

Looking back through my 1994 diary, the entries are filled with items like: "concrete yard, sort walls, paint doors, fix fridge floor, get quotes for moving fridge compressors up to roof," and so on. All worthy and mostly necessary work, but also expensive and time-consuming distractions from our core business, which still needed to generate the income to pay for it all—something the instigators of such regulations often seem oblivious to.

In September, I was presented with the DTI award, and the PR firm handling the event issued a press release explaining the award, its purpose, and who we were. This was reported in local papers— the Arran Banner and the Ardrossan and Saltcoats Herald—and even received brief mentions on BBC radio and television bulletins.

Receiving the Export Award Certificate

While several people, especially on Arran, offered genuine congratulations, not all responses were so generous. We had been working in the yard at Factory Place in Saltcoats for around five years by that point. The boys usually arrived around 8 a.m. to open up, and by 8:30 would often, though not always, have the forklift running, moving pallets of winkles in and out of the big fridge.

On days when a lot of business was expected, they might start a little earlier, especially if there were trucks waiting at the gate to be loaded. And although the forklift clattered across the yard, its electric motor was silent, and the overall noise level wasn't particularly high. Most days, everything was shut down by 5 p.m.

In those five years, no one had ever complained—at least not to us—about noise. But those who claim that all publicity is good publicity are probably unfamiliar with the mindset of a certain type of Scot: the kind permanently on a mission to protect his fellow countrymen from the danger of ever getting above themselves.

Roughly ten days after our export success was reported in the Ardrossan and Saltcoats Herald, a rather sheepish official from the Environmental Health Department arrived at the yard to inform us that they had received an anonymous complaint—of course—about noise from the yard during unsocial hours. Would we please try to do something about it?

We assured him that we would, and we never heard another word about it. Perhaps coincidentally, we were never featured in the local paper again. It would not be the last time anonymous complaints to officialdom caused us unnecessary grief.

Almost before we knew it, with all the focus on other matters, December rolled around again, bringing its usual mix of opportunity, pressure, and relentless work. With so much going on, Jan and I, as in previous years, based ourselves on the mainland for the busiest ten-day stretch.

Between the 10th and the 23rd, we bought and sold over 100 tons of winkles, for a monthly total of just over 198 tons. Every bag was paid for before Hogmanay, with a hope and a prayer that the invested money would return—with interest—within the first eight weeks of the new year.

Thankfully, it mostly did.

Chapter 14:

We were getting more and more winkles from Henry Donnelly in Ireland, so early in 1995 Jan and I went to Ireland to scout out any further possibilities, particularly in mussels, which were being farmed there in ever increasing quantities. Their markets were mainly in France, often to the same customers as we were selling winkles to, so on the surface it seemed like there could be possibilities there.

In practice, it turned out not to be so. The mussel farmers were well enough organised with customers whom they supplied directly, and the margins were so tight that there was no scope for another company to be profitably involved in the chain.

This idea of a chain—from producer or fisherman all the way through to the final consumer—is relevant all through the fishing industry and probably the entire food production industry, for that matter, as it illustrates the way in which markets become more and more efficient by gradually squeezing links out of the chain.

Taking the winkles as an example: when I first got into the industry back in 1985, there could be up to eight links in the chain between the winkle picker and the final consumer. The Arran pickers sold their winkles to buyers on the island, who then sold them to me, who then sold them to Primel, who then sold them to merchants in wholesale markets like Rungis in Paris, who then sold them to secondary wholesalers, who then sold them to fishmongers or supermarkets, who then sold them to consumers—or possibly to restaurants, who would cook them and sell them to their customers. All those people made a profit on the winkles, along with sundry hauliers who transported them between the various merchants.

But gradually, over time, as the market became more efficient, the number of links in the chain reduced until now anyone can sit at home and order winkles on the internet from a seller who may have bought them directly from the winkle pickers, thus cutting out all those links in the chain. That is a good illustration of how a market becomes efficient over time—by bringing the producer, in this case the fisherman or picker, closer to the final consumer by reducing the number of people making profit from the product.

We spent a lot of time in early 1995 looking for new markets and opportunities. We visited Portugal and found a few possible customers in a country we had previously ignored, but none of them came to anything, mainly through transport problems related to the relatively small quantities that would have been involved.

We also had a look at the south and south-east of France, mainly the Camargue region, where there was significant mussel farming and associated merchants, but there was little interest in winkles there. The small tidal range is not supportive of the common periwinkle. It has never been commercialised there, and we found little interest in it as a commercial product.

Another trawl around the French and Spanish Basque country proved more fruitful, and we picked up some customers for our crawled winkles in areas where we had no regular customers for the uncrawled product, so no political problems.

Seafish

The second half of the year was dominated by another regulatory problem which had arisen. Seafish, the industry body charged with promoting seafood, was proposing to levy all first buyers of seafood in order to fund their promotions.

They had worked out different rates of levy per kilo for all the different species which were commercially traded in the UK, roughly graded according to their first sale value. For reasons known only to themselves—and I never did find out why—they had classed winkles with prawns and lobsters, both of which were much higher value shellfish, to the extent of over ten-to-one in value in pounds per kilo, rather than with the much more similarly priced cockles, mussels, and oysters.

Furthermore, in the EC Health Regulations, winkles were subject to the same requirements as cockles, mussels, and oysters, rather than prawns and lobsters.

Once again, we appeared to be subject to incompetent and illogical legislation which had the potential to cost us a whole lot of money and cause us a world of trouble.

So I wrote to them explaining these facts and querying their thinking in choosing to do it that way, but got nowhere. Once again, I enlisted the help of the redoubtable Dr Eric Edwards of the Shellfish Association of Great Britain (SAGB). Eric knew exactly how to handle them and was highly skilled in negotiating the highways and byways of our governmental apparatus.

In the vernacular, Eric could speak to them "in their own lingo," and his softly-softly approach eventually persuaded them to see sense. Though I felt, as did many others, that we were being levied essentially to boost the sales of fish and chip shops, which while admirable enough, was of zero benefit to us.

Christmas 1995 was blighted by yet another series of French strikes, which, from November, created great uncertainty around orders and deliveries. This time the strikers were blockading transport hubs and distribution depots. This was a huge problem for everyone involved in the food industry at the most important time of the year, particularly those, like us, trading in perishable goods.

By this time the supermarkets had the vast majority of the food trade in France, and they were unwilling to give concrete orders to their suppliers as long as they were unable to be sure of getting the goods out of their distribution centres to the actual supermarkets. This uncertainty had a knock-on effect all the way down to the winkle pickers in Scotland and Ireland. Orders were "provisional," dependent on the strikers relenting and things going back to normal.

UK, French, and Spanish hauliers were also in an impossible position, unable to plan journeys through France, never mind to and from France, though the Spaniards had the alternative of bypassing France by taking direct ferries from England to Spain. Those ferries, however, were soon booked up.

Our problem was, like everyone else, we were dependent on the Christmas trade for our overall profitability for the year—our "fifth quarter." But if we got it wrong and bought expensive winkles at Christmas prices and couldn't get them sold, we would face a massive loss in January when we would have to sell them at massively reduced prices, if we could sell them at all. Not an enticing prospect.

I had to decide whether to buy as normal in the hope that the situation was resolved in time, or whether to cut back and play it safe. It was no consolation to know that many other people were in the same situation. Speaking to French customers and hauliers, the balance of opinion was that the French government would be under such huge pressure from the giants of the French supermarket industry to ensure a resolution that one would somehow be found.

So we carried on as close to normal as possible, and fortunately, around the end of the second week in December, it all calmed down and things were quickly back to normal—just in time. It was one of the most stressful periods of my time in the shellfish business, especially around the end of the first week of December when we had over 50 tons piled up in the fridge and another 50 bought and mostly paid for en route to Saltcoats from our suppliers all over the country, whom I had told to keep on buying.

In the end, we somehow managed to do just over 196 tons for the month.

1996

1996 was memorable for one event above all. On 19 March, our fourth child, Lauren, was born at the Queen Mother's Hospital in Glasgow.

Business continued, of course, but the weeks before and after Lauren's birth were dominated by it, and normal life only really resumed towards the end of summer while we adjusted to the changes in family life a new baby inevitably brings. And in a family business, changes in family life often mean changes in business life.

Fortunately, there were no extraneous factors involving bureaucratic agencies affecting us during that period. It was all quiet on the regulatory front, so we could concentrate on our new bundle of joy without any distractions other than normal business.

In any event, as years went, it was otherwise okay and uneventful. We sold just over 1,000 metric tons in the year, though our Christmas sales were down, partly thanks to yet more disruption in France, this time by truckers, which hurt our profitability for the year.

Little did I know as we brought in 1997, the kick in the teeth waiting for us just around the corner.

1997

Sometime in February 1997, one of our French customers rang me. "Had I heard? La Langouste had gone bust."

I hadn't heard, nor did I want to hear. They owed us £36,000.

It was the classic French shellfish trade move. Get in as much stock as you can for the Christmas sales frenzy, sell it all—mostly to supermarkets—get paid by them, then go bust.

I passed the details on to our debt collection agency, but I knew in my heart we'd be lucky to ever see a single Euro. And so it proved.

We had been lucky for a few years with only a few small bad debts, but our luck had run out and it felt pretty painful.

To further add to our misery that month, the French truckers' dispute reignited, disrupting business yet again.

In Spain, we had been working with two main customers, but the squeezing effect I spoke about earlier was now hitting them, and one of them was being forced out of the winkle business. Their modus operandi had worked very well for them for a long number of years, beginning long before I entered the industry.

They would place an order for usually a full artic load of 20 tons. When the truck arrived at their premises in Galicia, one of the directors would jump in the cab and take the driver around a series of small *depuradoras*, purification stations owned by different small merchants' businesses. At each *depuradora*, they would drop off whatever quantity of winkles the owners had ordered until the truck was empty, then back to base to drop off the director, the whole exercise taking no more than a couple of hours.

They knew all the small customers were good for the money, even if some might take a wee while to pay, while they themselves were excellent payers, always on time and rarely with any caveats. But lately, they had been finding that making their profit was more and more difficult. Their customers were getting offers from all over, and as the world shrunk and the market became more efficient, their margin had been squeezed to the point where it wasn't really worth their while bothering, since it was a very small part of their business, which was mainly in branded frozen seafood.

Their proposal was that we should deal directly with the small *depuradoras* ourselves, while they dropped out. I was happy to do this. It didn't really involve much more profit for us, and any increase was balanced out by the increase in risk through dealing with half a dozen people we were unfamiliar with rather than one highly dependable company, but it secured our sales in that part of the world, around the Rias Baixas of Galicia, one of the most important centres for shellfish in Spain.

The winkle market was changing. The price of winkles at Christmas had become so extreme that companies like our customers were adopting new, different strategies to avoid having to buy them at these prices. Some, those with seawater facilities and plenty of space, were stocking up from October onwards, just like we had been doing for a number of years. Some were buying when there was plenty of availability, and prices were even cheaper towards the end of summer.

Others, particularly in France, had replaced the winkles, which had gone from being a cheap filler on a *plateau de fruits de mer* (seafood platter), to being more expensive than oysters, with the much cheaper *bulot*, what we would call whelks (*Buccinum undatum*). So the overall demand for winkles in December had fallen. On top of that, there were not so many people picking winkles, so both supply and demand had diminished.

It made for a less hectic festive season, but also a less profitable one. And while to some, profit is a dirty word, for the private sector, it's what keeps the wolf from the door and ultimately, after it's been taxed, pays for all the public services that are sometimes taken for granted.

1997 also saw the latest scheme from Brussels to make our lives a misery, as they issued draft proposals for changes to the original shellfish regulations, which, since they had only been in operation for five years and hadn't caused any problems, obviously needed changing. Thus was our money spent, our lives made more difficult, and business disrupted by bureaucrats who appear to live in a world devoid of practicalities, preventing them from seeing the need to take practicalities into consideration.

The most contentious paragraphs in the draft legislation this time were again around labelling and referred to who exactly was *the gatherer*, what constituted *parcels of shellfish*, and the act of *placing on the market* those parcels. It was illustrative once again of how far removed from reality were the people drawing up these rules and regulations.

No allowance was still being made for the fact that much of the trade in shellfish was between merchants, rather than between an individual fisherman or fishing boat and a merchant, as described in a previous chapter. Nor was it acknowledged that, given these facts, no one involved in the industry was going to be happy passing on to their customer details of their supplier, as they were essentially being told to do—for the very obvious reason that their customer might seek to cut them out of any future business once in possession of those details.

George Golden of Carrowholly Shellfish put it well: "At the moment, 90% of the shellfish trade is fully legal and above board, and only about 10% isn't, but if they bring in their latest proposals without any changes, it will end up about exactly the other way round."

As we had come to understand, they would never admit to having issued bonkers proposals, but might turn a blind eye to *workarounds*, code for: "do it in the most sensible way possible which doesn't blatantly contravene the regulations but allows trade to continue." And after a lot of to-ing and fro-ing by a lot of concerned people in the UK and Ireland, that is what eventually happened.

The problem is, that's fine as long as nothing goes wrong, but if it does, you will probably find you're on your own.

1998

1998 began quietly and, much to our relief, without any more customers defaulting on the money we were owed. But it was just the calm before a different kind of storm.

Sometime in the first quarter of the year, Inland Revenue (IR) at Rothesay, our tax office, had requested sight of our books and records for the previous three tax years. This was concerning. I knew we had paid all the tax we were due, to the best of our knowledge, but I did have concerns about whether we might be accused of underpaying National Insurance (NI) at Troon, owing to our occasional payments to casual workers there who, despite our best efforts, steadfastly refused to furnish us with their P45s to enable us to put them "on the books."

Everyone at Saltcoats, in the office on Arran, and most at Troon were on the books with PAYE and NI deducted and returned to IR. But some of the Troon staff insisted they were self-employed and would deal with their own tax and National Insurance, though I suspected that for some at least, that would never happen—and IR would want us to pay it for them.

I wasn't unduly worried about it. It hadn't happened very often or for very long and shouldn't amount to much relative to the amounts of tax and NI we were paying.

Then, on 15 July, I received a letter addressed to me personally from the Inland Revenue, headed "Special Compliance Office Edinburgh." It was to inform me that SCO had commenced an investigation in respect of my tax affairs and the tax affairs of Sandy MacAlister Shellfish, and that they would be taking over the enquiries which had been conducted by IR Rothesay, our local tax office.

I was more curious than worried by this turn of affairs. I had never heard of the Special Compliance Office, knew nothing about them or what they did, other than that they were a different department within the Revenue. I remained in that innocent state for about an hour until I got a phone call from our accountant, Sandy Houston, who had also received a letter from SCO.

Sandy's response made me aware pretty quickly that this was a very big deal indeed. In Sandy's words, "These boys don't get out of bed unless they expect to find over £100,000 of unpaid income tax."

While what Sandy had said was chilling in its possible implications, in a strange way it was reassuring. It was so unrealistic to me to imagine that we could have been due over £100,000 *extra* income tax, on top of what I considered to be a humongous amount that we had paid in each of the years under investigation—and I *knew* that we had never defrauded anyone—that it must be down to some error in the IR system. It was just bizarre on so many levels. Bizarre or not, it would need to be dealt with, and the sooner the better.

Back in the early years of the business, when we began to handle large amounts of cash, it seemed inevitable to me that sooner or later Inland Revenue would take an interest in what we were doing, as they do with all businesses handling large amounts of cash, and that when they did, we would need professional assistance.

So I took out a policy with a company called IRPC, who specialised in providing legal advice and assistance to businesses in respect of various matters such as dealing with employment law, IR, Environmental Health, VAT, and many of the government departments and agencies which were often the bane of business people's lives.

I contacted IRPC and they allocated two of their team to our case—Peter Brown and Steve Norris—both ex-IR men who understood the ways of our antagonists. Peter and Steve got in touch, both with us directly and also with Sandy Houston. SCO had suggested a meeting on 28 July and had offered to meet at their offices, our office, our accountant's office, or anywhere else we wanted to meet.

Sandy advised we should meet them here at the farm. His reasoning was that it would let them see how we lived, that there was no evidence of conspicuous consumption or property improvements which might suggest suspicious sources of income over and above what we had declared, and also that it was an environment in which we would be as comfortable as you are ever likely to be in those circumstances. Sound advice. So we replied suggesting we meet them here on the 3rd of September, which would give Peter and Steve time to get up to speed on the details of our business and the particulars of the enquiry as it appeared to relate to our tax affairs.

Peter and Steve arrived on the island on the day before the meeting and went over our accounts with us that afternoon. They were reassuring, clearly knew their stuff, and were of the opinion that we had nothing to worry about.

That's easy to say—and the old cliché, "If you've got nothing to hide, you've got nothing to fear," doesn't offer much comfort when you ask yourself what on earth has triggered them investigating us at all, and for such apparently unrealistic amounts of money?

The meeting with SCO began around 10 o'clock the following morning, in the dining room of our house, which now served not for eating but as an office. We had moved the big table from the kitchen into the dining room. I was at the head of the table with my back to the window. The number two Revenue officer was at the opposite end. Jan and Peter were on one side of the table, and Steve and the lead taxman were on the other side.

The meeting began with introductions and then, as I believe is standard, with the lead taxman referring to the accounts we had submitted and asking if we had anything further to declare. I brought up the potential problem with the casual workers' National Insurance, but said that apart from that, I had nothing to add to the accounts they were in possession of.

There then began a couple of hours or so of probing by the two taxmen, obviously trying to trip us up in some way to confirm their evident suspicions. It felt a bit like the police turning up at your door and saying, "We think you've committed a murder." You might say in response, "Really? Who am I supposed to have murdered? Where and when did I do this?" "Ah, you tell us," would be all you would get in reply.

They were clearly working from some "information" they had garnered from somewhere—more likely someone. Peter and Steve had told us that most of these investigations began with an informant contacting Inland Revenue, usually anonymously, with some accusation of tax evasion. The usual suspects were disgruntled ex-partners—husbands or wives or business partners—or ex-employees with a grudge, or business competitors, jealous or suspicious neighbours. Quite a wide range of potential informants.

Peter and Steve had asked us if we thought we had any enemies who would go to these lengths to damage us or our business, but we thought that unlikely. We weren't aware of anything like that and had never been, nor felt, threatened by anyone at any time. As the meeting progressed, it became clear that they were definitely working from "information" supplied by someone.

There were two particularly chilling moments for me. The first was when they asked about a flat in Glasgow in which one of our daughters had lived for a time while at college in the city. The implication was that we might have bought this property, but I pointed out that we had never owned a property in Glasgow and she had only rented that flat during her time there. But, in any case, she had now left Glasgow.

"Yes, she's in Sydney now," said taxman number one, leaving both Jan and me open mouthed. How on earth did he know that? We both wondered simultaneously. She had only recently gone there, and even some of our family didn't know she was in Sydney.

"You're very well informed," I said. No response—just a slightly smug smile.

The second chilling moment, for me, came while taxman number one was asking Jan about some item or other in the accounts. I wasn't involved in the conversation and was just sitting, smiling benignly, while Jan explained some point he seemed to have difficulty understanding. When I glanced toward his colleague sitting directly across the table from me, his look wiped the smile from my face. He was staring at me intently, a look of pure concentration on his face, and it suddenly dawned on me—he was scrutinising me in what he thought was an unguarded moment to try and figure out if I was on the level or not. Not unlike the way, it occurred to me, that I would probably scrutinise a potential new customer in similar circumstances.

I don't think I have ever in my life been so conscious of my face falling, as I absorbed the unpleasant thought that my taxes were paying for this person to sit in my house trying to figure out if I was a crook or not.

The questions from the taxmen eventually came on to the subject of our Irish company, Carlingford Shellfish, and the nature of our relationship with it.

"Why did we set it up?"

I explained that in 1992, the UK government had begun consultations on the implementation of the proposed EC shellfish health regulations, due to come into effect in 1993. I explained that the way the UK authorities were proposing to implement the regulations (explained in an earlier chapter) had led me to believe that our business might become inoperable in the UK, so we needed to have an alternative prepared in case of that happening. So I had bought Paul Clark's business for £11,000 and formed Carlingford Shellfish with Paul's nephew, Henry Donnelly. I reminded them that they had had sight of a letter confirming this from Carlingford Shellfish's chartered accountant, as well as a full set of accounts for the Irish company.

Discussion on Carlingford Shellfish and our relationship with it went back and forth for quite a while, and I was struck by the assumptions and apparent low level of knowledge of the shellfish industry by the taxmen. I had been led to believe that when they investigated a pub or hotel or petrol station or newsagent, they knew exactly what profit "should" be getting made on every pound of turnover, so knew when the figures just didn't add up and tax was being evaded.

Their ignorance of our business, indeed the whole shellfish industry, appeared to be profound and spoke of not having done their homework before setting off on what, it was rapidly becoming clear, was no more than a fishing expedition.

I could be mistaken—their apparent lack of knowledge could have been a bluff. One of their questions was, "How much would a ton of winkles normally cost?" To which my answer was, "There's no such thing as normally. Depending on the time of the year, the size of the winkles, their quality and freshness, the state of the market, they could be anything from £300 to £2000."

The clue to their thinking came when taxman one said he was concerned about how I priced the Irish winkles. I said that I calculated the price we paid Carlingford Shellfish (CS) according to what the winkles had cost, while leaving enough on top to keep CS solvent after Henry had been paid.

"That just adds to my concerns," he said.

The only reason I could think of why he would have taken that attitude, in light of our puzzlement as to why he was investigating us at all, was that they suspected we were buying winkles in Ireland much more cheaply than in the UK but recording them at a false, much higher price and pocketing the difference—thus evading tax.

But there were no cheap winkles to be had in Ireland, North or South, as a call to the Revenue's Belfast office would have ascertained. There were plenty of other Irish companies involved with winkles, two or three of them major players, and selling into some of the same markets as we were at the same prices. It was a very competitive industry, and I was as concerned with some of them buying winkles through agents in Stranraer as no doubt they were about me buying them through Henry in Carlingford. The taxmen appeared not to have done their homework, instead setting off on a wild goose chase believing some nonsense given to them probably anonymously by a person or persons unknown, fuelled by jealousy or grievance or malice or all three.

It's telling that, throughout the entire two years and more it took to resolve this, Inland Revenue never produced a single piece of evidence which contradicted or even brought into question anything we had told them or submitted to them.

A lighter moment came when taxman two was looking at some papers which had been faxed to us from Carlingford. He suddenly got very excited and pointed out to me, with a note of triumph, that the fax header said "Sandy MacAlister Shellfish," which he clearly saw as evidence of some kind of malpractice. Jan gently pointed out to him that every document faxed to us from Carlingford had Sandy MacAlister Shellfish on the header—dozens of them—for the simple reason that I had given the fax machine to Henry when we bought a new one, and neither he nor I had any idea how to change the name on the header.

We then had to escort them around our house, letting them see into every room. I pointed out to them that all the decades-old sash windows remained in place, no double glazing, some of the woodwork rotten and needing replacement—basically unchanged from before we had started the shellfish business. Disappointment at that may have been a contributory factor in their evident excitement when we showed them the one room in the house we had spent money improving. In the bathroom, we had recently installed a spa bath, a wall heater, and new sanitaryware and tiling. Exclamations of "Ah" betrayed their feelings, which were somewhat dampened when we told them that it had all been paid through the bank and the invoices and receipts were all available downstairs for them to scrutinise if they wanted—though for reasons known only to themselves, they declined this offer.

Eventually, the meeting drew to a close with the taxmen no further forward than they had been at the beginning. Of course, they weren't going to admit that, so they decided that we had to have a comprehensive audit done of our accounts for the years under investigation. Inland Revenue could do it, or we could have it done by Steve or Peter, all at our expense. Naturally, as we had the insurance cover for Steve and Peter, we opted for one of them to do the audit.

Nothing good happens quickly with Inland Revenue, and by the time Peter had done the audit—with all the back and forth with the Revenue that it involved—over two years had passed since the start of the investigation. Finally, we got the outcome.

For the casual labour employees' NI underpayments we had flagged up at the start of the meeting, we were charged a back payment of a few thousand pounds, with a ten percent penalty. That small penalty of only ten percent, Steve and Peter informed us, was the nearest thing you will ever get to an apology from Inland Revenue. Normally, after such an investigation, any unpaid tax would be liable to a fifty or one hundred percent penalty, even more in really egregious cases. They reckoned the cost to the Revenue of the investigation would have been in the region of £100,000, for essentially no more return than Rothesay office could have got with a couple of letters—illustrating the dangers of believing malicious tittle-tattle contrary to any evidence.

One good thing to come out of the whole farrago was my realisation of how exposed we were from handling so much cash—something I dealt with within a few days of the SCO meeting. I made it clear to everyone we bought from that we would no longer be paying cash for winkles. All payments would be through the bank. We lost a few suppliers, but most accepted it, and within a month we had completely eliminated cash from the business.

What I had realised at the SCO meeting was how incredibly vulnerable buying and paying with cash made us. I could draw £1,000 from the bank to pay someone for winkles and enter it in our accounts. But they might decide to keep £300 off the books for themselves and enter it as having received only £700. If the Inland Revenue happened to compare the two sets of accounts, it would be clear to them that someone wasn't telling the truth. They might not know whose accounts were false, but they would know that someone's were—and would probably assume both were.

That was a risk I no longer wished to take, and I never regretted that decision.

It pains me to admit it, but those years of worry and stress, during and after the investigation, temporarily knocked the stuffing out of me. The whole affair was deeply unsettling. It's difficult to explain adequately the way it makes you feel knowing that people are sitting in offices in Glasgow or Edinburgh discussing whether or not you're a criminal and how they can prove that you are, on the basis of nothing more than anonymous tittle-tattle—either malicious or misinformed or both—from a person or persons unknown to them but almost certainly known to you. It's no consolation to know that they were just doing their job as they saw it and that ultimately they had to admit defeat. When you're the subject of their investigations, the process you have to undergo is its own punishment, even when you're innocent.

We felt violated and extremely bitter about it at the time and for a long time afterwards—and to a certain extent, I still do. That bitterness was fuelled not just because of Inland Revenue's investigation of our business without any actual hard evidence, but, by way of contrast, their apparent reluctance to pursue multinational corporations with similar vigour. During the nineties there were many credible allegations about the reluctance of Inland Revenue to tackle tax avoidance—and worse—by some of the biggest corporations in the world. Yet on the basis of apparently nothing more than anonymous hearsay, they subjected us to over two years of stress and worry, apparently for trying to expand our business by trading in Ireland, to the benefit, ultimately, of the UK exchequer and balance of payments.

It bears repeating that Inland Revenue were unable to produce a single piece of evidence which contradicted or brought into question any of our tax returns, our figures, or our testimony during the entire duration of their investigation.

For a long time after it was all over, I found it impossible to "take the positives and move on," as the sportspeople say. It would take the arrival of our daughter Louise as a partner in the business a few years later to re-energise me. But for a few years after the tax case concluded, my interest in further growth of the business was non-existent. We concentrated on maintaining our winkle business at the same level as previously, which we were able to do with only a few forays into other products like cockles and mussels, for which we installed a brand new purification system at Saltcoats. We also adapted this for crawling winkles, as we had lost the premises at Troon, damaged so severely in the Boxing Day storm of 1998 that ABP had no interest in repairing them. In any case, they had other plans for that area of the harbour—a new ferry service to Northern Ireland.

We were fairly successful, with an unbroken run of sales of over £1 million a year, mostly exports, from 1999 to 2012.

For anyone not au fait with the language of business, I should stress that sales are not profit. Sales, in a trading business like ours, basically translate into turnover, and as Duncan Bannatyne was fond of pointing out on the Dragons' Den TV programme, "turnover is vanity, profit is sanity." Fortunately, we never had an unprofitable year, though it always amazed winkle pickers who would often ask me how much we made on a bag of winkles. When I replied, around £1.50 to £2 after tax, they were surprised. They knew what I was paying them and they'd heard what the price of winkles was in foreign markets and usually assumed that we were making a lot more than that. But what they had no idea of were the costs of running the business and getting the winkles to those foreign markets—wages, transport, bags, pallets, electricity, repairs and maintenance, bad debt, waste, insurance, bank interest and so on. Not to mention the costs involved in keeping multiple similar but slightly different records.

For instance, we had to keep an accurate record of all our buying and selling in the normal way of all businesses for HMRC, as the Revenue and VAT people are now called. For Environmental Health, we had to keep records of all our buying, where they came from, where they had gone, and to whom, along with movement documents with the details of each consignment. Also, risk assessments for every action involved in doing that. For Intrastat, an

EC body, we had to keep another set of records detailing the value of all our exports to EC countries and the VAT numbers of each customer. For the Seafish Levy people, we had to keep records of who we had bought each batch of shellfish from and the species, differentiating which buys were from agents and which were direct from fishermen, calculate what levy was due on them and pay them the levy. Because we ran Heavy Goods Vehicles, we had to keep records of them and their maintenance and also the drivers' hours. I imagine today there might be a computer programme into which you could input all those details and let it sort out the results in the appropriate agencies' forms. It all had to be done and kept up to date and available for inspection by the relevant agency, and doing that cost money and brought no little aggravation from time to time if an inspection revealed something not completely up to date or in contravention of some regulation or other.

In any case, not long after the conclusion of the tax case, family problems intervened and deflected my attention back to cattle and sheep alongside the shellfish business for a few years. Cleaning up behind cows' tails was a part of my life again, though at least this time from a tractor seat pulling a scraper, rather than with a shovel and a barrow, in the firing line so to speak. In days of yore, the barrow had to be pushed up a midden plank several times a day. A midden is a dung heap, a midden plank is a wooden plank broad enough to push a wheelbarrow up to the top of the midden, there to dump the contents of the barrow.

Chapter 15:

The financial crisis of 2008 hit the European shellfish sector, like most other sectors, pretty hard. Businesses were closing down or cutting back, bad debt was on the rise, and everyone was wary of risk in a way they hadn't been before. It looked to me like the future was more likely to lie in the Far East than in Europe, as we kept hearing about the buoyancy of markets in Hong Kong and Singapore despite the financial problems of the rest of the world.

I wrote earlier about an unthinkable postscript to my relationship with the Bank of Scotland, and this was another consequence of the financial crisis. As banks' share prices collapsed and banks previously thought to be "as safe as houses" went bust, we had by then achieved a position of financial stability such that I felt we had more reason to be concerned about their creditworthiness than they had about ours. So when someone from BOS Head Office requested what security we might offer for a small overdraft, for an enterprise unrelated to the shellfish business, I felt entirely justified in pointing out that, given that they already held the title deeds to almost all of my property assets and were custodians of a six-figure sum of my money, in the current climate perhaps that question might be more appropriately addressed from me to them, since at that time only around £32,000 was covered by the FSCS guarantee. A bit cheeky maybe, but in light of the situation, understandable.

I had been contacted previously by razor clam fishermen in the Clyde asking if I had any interest in their product, which at that time I hadn't, since I knew nothing about razor clams and was focused only on keeping my head down and getting on with what I knew worked. However, after Louise joined us, with all the enthusiasm and energy of youth, she was keen to give it a go, so we started buying razors in a small way.

Originally we were buying from boats fishing off Kintyre, which in the beginning involved Louise driving an old Volvo estate car round to Carradale every night to pick up their catch. Eventually, we arranged to load their catch onto the truck of a haulier, Peter McConnochie, who would drop them off for us at the Glasgow Fish Market. Louise, who was then living in Glasgow, would pick them up early in the morning and bring them back to Saltcoats for packing, taking them back to dispatch centres in the Glasgow area on her way home, along with any winkles sold that day.

After a while, we were contacted by a Hong Kong buyer of razor clams who had heard we were now in the razor business—Ricky Tsai—so I went to Hong Kong to meet him and see his operation. Incidentally, my flights on that trip were paid for by Scottish Enterprise, the only public money the business ever received in its 35-year existence, though Jan paid her own way with Avios vouchers she'd been collecting for years.

Hong Kong was fascinating, in particular the apparent difference between their level of hygiene regulation and ours, although since

China has taken over, much may have changed. The sheer energy of the city was incredible, with almost everyone moving around the streets as if they'd just escaped a burning building, and tower blocks built so close together you could almost imagine jumping across from one to the other.

I agreed to send as many large and medium-sized razors as possible to Ricky, and we had a few years of mutually profitable business before bureaucracy intervened and finished the razor business for us. On our return from Hong Kong, we set about increasing our supply of razors, which meant either persuading more fishermen to change to razors or persuading more existing razor fishermen to sell to us rather than their existing buyers.

In this we were moderately successful, and owing to the greater profitability on a per-kilo basis of the razor clams compared to the winkles, the main focus of the business shifted from the winkles to the razors. This reduced our sales volume in sterling but increased our profitability. The continuing malaise in European markets and the relative strength of Hong Kong and Singapore, where we had also picked up a couple of customers, and also increasing demand for razor clams here in the UK, strengthened the case for the razors over the winkles, for which there was no profitable market in Asia.

My life became a bit different during the razor years. Our customers were in the UK, France, Spain, Hong Kong, Singapore, Shanghai, and—through one of our UK customers—Malaysia and Thailand. The Asian customers were serviced by air from Glasgow

Airport, usually though not always via Heathrow. The European customers were serviced by road with consignments most days, which needed to be delivered to the various transport hubs around Glasgow, along with the UK consignments, which went out most days of the week except Sunday.

It was very much an early morning game. Louise, living in Glasgow, would be up and out by 6 a.m. and picking up the razors fished the previous day, which Peter McConnochie's truck had dropped off through the night. She would be back at Saltcoats with the razors sorted and weighed by around 8 a.m. I would have known the night before what should be there from talking to the skippers after they finished fishing, but it was important to confirm the weights as early as possible so any mix-ups could be sorted quickly before the dispatch orders were confirmed.

Louise and the Saltcoats team would then get started packing the orders, which I would have finalised and faxed through after confirming that the quantities we were expecting had in fact arrived. It sounds simple enough, but it was far from simple. My day would have actually started the evening before, when I spoke to the skippers and found out what I would have available to sell the following morning. From that, I would guesstimate what orders I was likely to get in the morning and tentatively allocate so many of this size and so many of that size to this customer, then so many of this size and so many of that size to that customer, and so on until I had allocated everything and, hopefully, had a clearance—at least on paper.

Easy enough, just so long as the customers ordered what I expected them to order in the morning, and what arrived from the boats was what had been promised. Because of the different time zones—the Far East customers were seven hours ahead of us—though their consignments wouldn't arrive at their local airport until the following day, usually for selling the day after that, and the fact that the UK customers were doing their selling in real time, as it were, for delivery to their customers through the following night for the next morning's market, I needed to be at my desk and ready to sell by 7 a.m., hoping that what I'd been told would be arriving by the skippers the night before actually turned up. Which meant, in practice, I had to be at my desk by 6 a.m. to assess what we had, including hearing from Louise if she had encountered any problems with her pickups.

To add another layer of complexity, I would usually have orders for our most valuable Far East customer, Ricky, for the following day's dispatch. I might need to keep some back if today's fishing looked like it would be disappointing, which I probably wouldn't know until after they'd started packing at Saltcoats. It was important too to make sure what fishing our most important skipper, Neil Urey—whose boat Wendy Liam was the mainstay of our supply— was expecting for that day and the next. My aim was always to try to ensure every customer got what they wanted and was happy, so they were likely to keep coming back, while keeping waste to an absolute minimum. This was more difficult with the razors than the winkles, due to their much shorter lifespan once out of the water. The reward was greater, but so was the risk, so the risk-to-reward metric balanced out. It was just as important that the fishermen were happy, as they also had plenty of alternatives to dealing with us, just like the customers.

Gradually, I began getting up earlier and earlier until I drew a line at 4 a.m. as the earliest I was going to set my alarm. That became my standard working day starting time, a habit I've continued into retirement, with working on buying and selling razors being replaced by time on an exercise bike, followed by a shower and another couple of hours of sleep.

Once all the day's orders were packed, Louise would take them up to the various dispatch centres around Glasgow before going home for the day. Meanwhile, Jan and Marion in the office would write up the delivery notes and we'd fax them to the relevant dispatch centre ahead of Louise getting there. I would then price up the invoices and fax them to each customer, which concluded the day's sales—usually by mid-afternoon. Then came a few hours of relaxation before it all began again in the early evening, as the boats we were buying from phoned with their news of how the day's fishing had gone.

It sounds more straightforward than it was because of three main factors. The first was the weather. A boat could set off early in the morning, predicting they should have thirty boxes by night time, which you would then factor into your planning. A couple of hours later, after you had provisionally sold these boxes, the skipper could be back on the phone to tell you they were on the fishing grounds but the weather was too poor for the divers to go down. So they were coming back in, and your thirty boxes wouldn't be arriving after all.

Then there was equipment failure, always a potential problem on any fishing boat. And then there were the divers. Most of the skippers were the kind of guys who just got on with the job, whatever obstacles were in their path, day after day, as long as the weather was good and there were no breakdowns. The divers, referred to by some skippers as prima donnas, were a different breed. Some occasionally failed to turn up, particularly after a couple of good days. Others would lay down the law on what they would and wouldn't do. This was a particular problem if the skipper thought the weather was fine but the divers disagreed—though you couldn't blame them for that, given the nature of their work.

Then there were the skippers who hedged their bets, selling to a variety of customers of whom we were just one. On days when you had a lot of orders expected and not much likely supply from your regular boats, you might ask one of these guys to send you as much as they could. They'd tell you they didn't think they could spare you more than half a dozen boxes, only to call in the evening with the good news that they were sending you forty boxes—their regular buyer obviously had too many. This sometimes happened just before your biggest customer called to cancel a big order because there was a typhoon coming. That was always bad news in Hong Kong, especially if you were committed to buying expensive razors for that market which you would now struggle not to sell but just to get rid of as best you could. And it had been one of the hottest days of the summer, so the razors wouldn't have a very long life in them after lying on the deck in the sun most of the day with only the occasional hosing with seawater to cool them down.

The customers had their difficulties too. If I was sitting in my office early on Monday morning taking orders, the UK customers were calculating what supply they needed for Tuesday. The French customers needed to work out what they needed for Wednesday when they would be selling my Monday dispatch. The Far East customers also had to work out their Wednesday sales before ordering, as their Monday dispatches were going by air. The Spanish customers had the toughest calculation of all, as they wouldn't be selling our Monday dispatch until Thursday, possibly even later.

Keeping suppliers happy was just as important as keeping customers happy, so you would just have to get on with dealing with the mess you sometimes inadvertently created for yourself. I lost count of the number of times something happened—like putting the phone down having been told something would happen that neatly tied in with something else you'd already arranged, such as a big order matching a big landing—only to get another call an hour later that blew up one half of the equation. You would then face the unpleasant task of telling someone something they didn't want to hear or contemplating the probability of losing a chunk of money, or both.

We couldn't have made a success of the razors without Louise's hard work and attention to detail and having her there, meant I had someone who knew the job from both sides and who I could trust implicitly to do my job, which allowed me the luxury of a worry-free break from time to time.

Buying and selling razors and getting it right was just about the most mentally challenging thing I've ever done, but I loved it. If I am good at anything, I like to think I have a talent for "guesstimation"—the mental juggling of various unpredictable events into a reasonably accurate guess as to the final outcome. The feeling of achievement when, despite all the hurdles, you managed to match up razors from four or five different boats with the exact or nearly exact orders from ten or so customers, knowing that all involved—suppliers and customers—were happy, was brilliant. Some may find that sad, but trust me, you had to be there.

Of course, I didn't always get it right. Which is partly why my years in the shellfish business have convinced me that one of the key skills in running any successful enterprise—be it a business, political office, or any environment where personal relationships are key—is the ability to tell people things they don't want to hear while still maintaining a good relationship with them. It was something I frequently had to do, though not always as successfully as I would have hoped.

However, for us, the razor years came to an end in 2015. There had for years been contention between the fishermen and Marine Scotland, the authority with responsibility for fishing matters in Scottish waters, about the legality of the method of fishing used by the razor fishermen. It was claimed that some boats were using electricity generated on board to assist the divers in releasing the razors from their burrows in the sand, making collection easier. This resulted in an ongoing contest between some fishing boats and Marine Scotland's fisheries protection vessels, as the authorities tried to catch them in the act of using electricity.

We were not affected directly by this, as there was no prohibition on buying razors, no matter how they had been fished. The dived razors were of far better quality and had a longer life than those that had been dredged, so practically all Scottish razors were dive caught.

Then around 2014, we began to hear rumours that Marine Scotland (MS) were planning to change the law to make it an offence to land razor clams without a licence to do so and also to buy them from any boat without a licence, which would definitely affect us. Licences would be issued to certain boats to trial fishing with electricity. A trial was eventually organised but only began in 2018 and continues at the time of writing, May 2025.

Matters came to a head when MS introduced a permit system without which it would be illegal to have any razor clams on board a boat at any time. That decided the main boats we had been working with to give up razor fishing and turn to other, more traditional species.

By this time, with all the uncertainty around the direction fishing for razors would take, Louise had decided to go in a different direction. She returned to Arran and opened a restaurant in partnership with a friend. So we ended our involvement with razor clams, and Jan and I continued selling winkles, though on a much smaller scale, with only one man employed at Saltcoats. I would go over once a week, sort out the orders, and take them up to the distribution depots around Glasgow.

I continued working this way until February 2021, when I had a stroke which incapacitated me for a few weeks. Further investigations after a brain scan discovered I'd had two mini strokes previously. These had not displayed the classic stroke symptoms of slurred speech or facial distortion and revealed that I have atrial fibrillation (AF), an irregular heartbeat which apparently increases susceptibility to strokes.

At the end of December 2020, I had told my customers and suppliers that I would be doing no business in the following month, January 2021. This was because we were finally Brexiting on 1 January, and I expected transport would probably be a bit chaotic for a few weeks until things settled down. We hadn't got back into action before the stroke hit, and after I had recovered from that—given the discovery of the two previous mini strokes and the AF—plus the fact I had just had my 71st birthday, I reluctantly came to the conclusion that it was probably time to close the shellfish business.

I've never been a religious believer, but when I added it all up, it seemed a wee bit like I was being sent a message: time to call it a day. So I sold the van, the yard, and all the equipment and ended my thirty-five and a half years in the shellfish industry—almost exactly half my lifetime at that time.

Epilogue

Some people may have noticed how few photos there are of the people, places, and events described here. That's because it never occurred to me, or anyone else involved, to take photos while we were running the business. We hadn't the time anyway, and I never once imagined that in my seventies, I would be writing a book about the greater part of my working life or would wish I had thought to take a few photos of the people and places involved.

Many people on Arran had never heard of our business. A few people knew that we bought a few wilks and had a yard in Saltcoats, but beyond that, few had any idea what our business was about. It would probably have been different if the line of vehicles laden with wilks in the street outside the Saltcoats yard most days of the week had been on the String road outside our farm, or if the two or three forty-foot refrigerated trucks, which arrived empty and departed fully loaded most Saturdays, had been coming and going on the Ardrossan to Brodick boat. But doing any more than the office work from Arran was inconceivable owing to the extra costs involved and the inadequacies of the ferry service, much as we would have preferred to do it all from home.

We rarely volunteered any information about our business locally, despite always answering any questions we were asked about it—though that rarely happened—because most people who knew of the existence of the business were just not much interested in what we were doing. Arran is sometimes described as "Scotland in Miniature," and it is, in more than just geology and beautiful scenery. "Blowing your own trumpet" is not really appreciated. I remember once listening to a "Mate" (the merchant navy rank) on the Ardrossan boat talking about what the people in Lamlash were saying about him. Also listening was a Lamlash resident who commented to me later, "Hhmm, naebody in Lamlash even knows he exists."

I just wanted a more financially secure future for my family, and in pursuing that, everything described above followed. I hope that most people will see it primarily as an illustration of what can be achieved by a positive attitude and a spirit of enterprise, though I have always appreciated that not everyone has the good fortune I had in owning the farm which was the bank's collateral for all the borrowing I needed.

My positive attitude was not something inherent. I developed it over time after a period of self-analysis, during which I came to the conclusion that I was too inclined towards negativity, too prone to focusing on what could go wrong rather than how to make things go right. It wasn't possible to totally banish negativity, but over time, I gradually developed the confidence to overcome the many challenges the business threw up.

In taking on the rest of the established winkle industry in Scotland and Ireland, an industry I knew nothing about, I had one advantage. Thanks to the hard work of my father and mother, and due to my father's untimely death and the idiosyncrasies of Scots inheritance law, I could give the bank the security without which they would never have been prepared to finance my plans, or might have taken fright at some stage and pulled the plug, destroying the business.

I exploited that advantage to the max and was able to create a business which, whilst directly employing no more than five to fifteen people at any one time, nevertheless provided all or part of the rewards for the fruits of the labour of literally hundreds of winkle pickers every year for thirty-five years.

To do what we did, I had to "bet the farm," an Americanism defined as "to risk everything that one owns on a bet, investment or enterprise." If a few of our biggest customers had defaulted simultaneously, we would have been in serious, probably terminal, trouble financially. Had that happened, I would have been, perhaps justifiably, open to accusations that I "couldn't run a whelk stand"— Britain's favourite shorthand for someone commercially clueless. I took a calculated risk, backing my judgment that our main customers were sound and extremely unlikely to let us down, that our basic ratio of risk to reward was favourable, and that consequently, the business rested on solid foundations and was therefore unlikely to come to grief.

In any case, I understood that risk is the price you often have to pay for the opportunity to prosper, and I accepted that risk. In the words of one of my sporting heroes, Shane Warne, "You have to be fearless and back yourself at all times." I've certainly never been fearless, and I don't always have the courage to back myself, but in this instance, I was convinced I was right and would come out ahead in the end.

That we did was thanks to many people, too numerous to mention them all, but especially everyone we employed at Saltcoats, Troon, and on Arran; (most of) our customers; all our loyal pickers and suppliers, especially Henry Donnelly, Carel Goodheir, Bryan Starmer and the late Colin Oman; my wife and business partner Jan, without whose hard work, checking, checking, checking, and constant support, it would never have happened; and my late brother Charlie whose careful management of the farm business, allowed me to create and run the business described in this book.

www.ingramcontent.com/pod-product-compliance
Lightning Source LLC
Chambersburg PA
CBHW051155120626
46547CB00012B/1077